Edna Aizenberg

Parricide on the Pampa?

Alberto Gerchunoff: from the 1936 edition of *Los gauchos judíos*

Edna Aizenberg

Parricide on the Pampa?
A New Study and Translation of
Alberto Gerchunoff's *Los gauchos judíos*

Vervuert • Iberoamericana • 2000

Photos courtesy of the Photo Archive, Mark Turkow Center for the Study of Argentine Jewry, Asociación Mutual Israelita Argentina (AMIA), Anita Weinstein, Director. Reprinted with permission.

Die Deutsche Bibliothek – CIP-Einheitsaufnahme

Ein Titeldatensatz für diese Publikation ist bei Der Deutschen Bibliothek erhältlich

ISBN 84-95107-74-0 (Iberoamericana)
ISBN 3-89354-121-7 (Vervuert)

Depósito Legal: NA-2108/2.000

Cubierta: Gustavo Antonio Asuar Coupe
Impreso en España por: Digitalia, S.L.
Este libro está impreso íntegramente en papel ecológico sin cloro.

INDEX

Acknowledgments

This book is the result of many years of thinking about the Jewish gauchos. It gestated over two decades ago in Ana María Barrenechea's seminar on the *gauchesca*, and it matured in a variety of propitious settings –lectures in the Moisesville library, seminars at Yale, and articles in *The New York Times*. My special thanks to the National Endowment for the Humanities for supporting my pampean research; to Benjamin Harshav of Yale University for stimulating my meditations on Gerch and his work; to David Roskies, Ismar Schorsch, Zvia Ginor, and Jack Wertheimer for the opportunity to share my Russo-Judeo-Argentine ruminations with the students at JTS; to Alicia Borinsky (Boston University) and Marcus Bullock (University of Wisconsin) for inviting me to speak and write about *los gauchos judíos*; to Daniel Walden (Penn State) for reading the manuscript and making cogent suggestions; to my *colegas y amigos* in Buenos Aires, Anita Weinstein, Eliahu Toker, and Ricardo Feierstein; to Regina Peruggi, President of Marymount Manhattan College, for a sabbatical leave which gave me time to prepare the study; to my publisher, Klaus Dieter Vervuert, for his persistence, to Ronja A. Matuschek, for her editing, and to Stanley Berkson, computer wizard. To the people of Moisesville, who opened their homes to me on those cold pampa mornings and allowed me to experience *lo que es y lo que fue*. To my family and, as always, to Joshua, with love.

Gerchunoff's entire work deserves to be translated... Because you can find bits and pieces of him in every one of his writings, in every sentence... When I think about him, what comes to mind is not a book or a page of a book, but something much more important –the man Gerchunoff... That's why I like to remember him, I like to talk about him, I like to transmit my feelings to others.

Jorge Luis Borges

INTRODUCTION

> I pick up *The Jewish Gauchos* once again. I reread the book, nostalgically reliving each of its pages. I see my father's comments written in the margins, and my comments under his. So many decades come alive, so many memories, so many echoes shaking me to the core... As I close the beloved book, I am moved to tears by this testimony to our youth and to the magic of the new land.
>
> *Lázaro Liacho*

> What is the meaning of [Gerchunoff's] bucolic Argentina in the face of... the violent Argentina of the Buenos Aires pogroms?
>
> *David Viñas*

This book inspires strong passions. At first read, it seems an unlikely candidate for such outbursts of emotion. *The Jewish Gauchos* is a collection of twenty-three stories about turn-of-the-century Jewish immigrants to the Argentine pampa authored by one of their own, the Russian-born Alberto Gerchunoff. Gerchunoff began to publish vignettes based on his country life in 1908. These sketches, some first printed in the influential Buenos Aires daily, *La Nación*, became the seed of *Los gauchos judíos*, which appeared as a volume two years later.

If the genesis and content of Gerchunoff's work are as bland as the bare-bones outline, then why the fuss? Why the powerful reactions, the virulently opposing opinions, the heated critical discussions, the many reprintings and imitations, this new study and translation? Readers of Gerchunoff's better-known countryman, Jorge Luis

Borges, might recall the acrimonious debates surrounding that author's work, the longstanding arguments between the adherents of the "good" Borges whose fictions helped remake contemporary literature, and the enemies of the "bad" Borges who escaped the realities of his nation (see Aizenberg 1997). But Gerchunoff?

The controversies about Gerchunoff are less familiar, but in this era of fierce disputes about immigration and multiculturalism, it is high time for an English-speaking audience to become acquainted with his creation. Borges's *El Aleph* (1949) may be the most famous "Jewish" book to come out of the republics of the south, yet Gerchunoff's was a precursor text. Much before Borges, the agriculturalist-turned-writer posed important questions about literature written at the crossroads of tradition and modernity, and displayed the problematic multicultural layering since considered characteristic of the best Latin American fiction.

On the brink of the twentieth century, Gerchunoff –a colorful figure in Buenos Aires literary and journalistic circles, a founder of the Argentine Writers' Association, a defender of Borges, and a friend of Rubén Darío, Leopoldo Lugones, and other Latin American literary lions– presented sociocultural dilemmas common to both Americas: How do you negotiate the breach between the demands of homogeneity and the need to sustain ethnic identity? How do you open up histories, ideologies, and literary canons? How do you constitute culture on the periphery and resist the forces of authoritarianism and prejudice?

Gerchunoff asked these questions at the century's opening, hopeful about its possibilities. Now that it has closed, still struggling with the predicaments he experienced, it is appropriate to let his inaugural book speak to a broad readership that includes, in North America and elsewhere, large Hispanic and Jewish communities, as well as other minority and immigrant groups. At a moment when writers are struggling to create modes of expression that do not hide ethnic or sexual difference, his book addresses the difficulties inherent in any reductionist view of community and self (see Foster).

The Context of a Canonical Text

The story of Gerchunoff's pathbreaking words begins with prior words, found in the Argentine constitution of 1853: "The Federal Government will encourage European immigration, and will in no way... restrict... the entry into Argentine territory of foreigners whose aim is to work the land, improve industry, and introduce the arts and sciences." A radical departure from colonial Spain's closed-door policy in Latin America, the declaration embodied the desire of independent Argentina's nation builders to "govern by populating" –to fill their country's vast, unharnessed spaces with hardworking immigrants whose European habits and skills would lift the land out of its "barbarism" into "civilization."

This unabashedly Eurocentric modernization project called for the extermination of the Native Americans and the domestication of the gaucho, the free-riding cowboy of the pampa, whose wild ways no longer suited an Argentina intent on becoming a progressive member of the concert of nations. "Peace and prosperity" meant closely tying Argentina to Europe, but not as an industrial partner, as an exporter of meat and wheat; this longterm weakness was overlooked in the rush for modernization.

Riddled with contradictions, the modernization program did nonetheless succeed in imposing its model on reality, changing the demographic face of Argentina and fostering greater economic well-being. By 1910, year of the first centennial of Argentine independence, the country's leaders could boast that the nation had become a prosperous melting pot in which people of diverse backgrounds were amalgamated harmoniously. The price paid by minorities for such "amalgamation," and the fissures in the smooth façade –labor strikes, anti-immigrant pogroms– were scarcely mentioned.

The words of the 1853 constitution were broadcast by emissaries sent from the far-off New World to the Old. They found a ready audience in Baron Maurice de Hirsch, the Judeo-Belgian philanthropist anxious to undertake a civilizing mission of his own –the saving of his Jewish brethren from the barbarism of the Russian Pale. Under his auspices, starting in 1891, the Jewish Colonization Association (ICA) began to purchase acreage on the pampa in order to settle Jews; Moisesville was the first colony to be established.

In fact, just as Argentina's immigration policies were an attempt to move away from Hispano-Catholic feudalist pastoralism, so was the baron's plan part of the modernization of Jewish life. From the beginning of the last century, the Jewish world had undergone radical transition from a "medieval" to a modern existence, as Jews, impelled by czarist anti-Semitism and diminishing economic horizons, emigrated by the millions to North and South America. The period saw an expansion of traditional Jewish culture, anchored in the Hebrew Scriptures, with new secular literatures in Hebrew, Yiddish, and European languages. Jews adopted new ideologies of action –Zionism, Socialism, Territorialism– that contrasted profoundly with religious teachings fostering obedience to God and faith in His redemption.

The intersection of the two modernization processes, Jewish and Argentine, had a particular coloring, significant for understanding Gerchunoff. These were modernizations on the margin, of peoples in ambiguous relationships with the centers of Western culture. At the turn of the century, Jews –the quintessential minority– and Argentines, long colonized by Spain, both had an uncertain territoriality, an undefined linguistic-cultural identity, and a murky ideological field, in which newer forces of pluralism struggled mightily with older exclusivist models.

Like many postcolonial peoples, the Argentines had only recently unified their national space and were struggling to cohere a physical and imagined community called "Argentina." Building an identity was a fundamental aspect of this task: If Argentines were no longer subjects of Spain yet continued to speak Spanish, how should their language differ? And what should they do about the languages of the immigrants flooding the country? Should Argentine identity be based on the fast-disappearing Hispanic ruralist model, symbolized by the landowner and the gaucho, or was it to be a Europeanized, urban identity? Were the literary paradigms to remain gauchesque literature, poetry and prose based on the exploits of the gaucho, such as José Hernández's master poem, *Martín Fierro* (1872), or were newer forms, often inspired by continental fashions, to prevail? Did the coming of the foreigners signal greater openness in the political system, or could the country continue to be governed in oligarchic style?

Jews, for their part, were even more unsure as they entered modernity. Exiled for two thousand years, they had no territory at all. The major ideologies of the period contended with this vital problem, made desperately acute by the latest round of czarist pogroms. Zionism proposed the establishment of a Jewish home in the ancestral Promised Land; Socialism aimed at Jewish normalcy through a juster order wherever Jews lived; Territorialism sought to end dispersal anywhere –for instance, in agricultural colonies on the pampa. A literal, regenerating "living on the land" was an integral part of the ideological effervescence. Jews became farmers and a more urban folk at one and the same time.

Cultural-linguistic disputes were likewise heated. Was Yiddish, the idiom of Eastern European Jewry, to be the modern Jewish tongue? Or was it Hebrew, the scriptural language that had united all Jews? What about the European languages, which Jews increasingly made their own? And as Jews integrated into society, to what extent should they abandon their relatively closed, traditional communities and "melt" into the secularized, though still Christian environment? The issue was of great consequence, since secularism and integration exacted a price seen in the existential anguish of those who abandoned old ways without being totally accepted by society, and in the diminution of strongly-marked Jewish identity.

Territory, language, ideology –the similar challenges that faced Jews and Argentines did not, however, make for an easy coexistence; more often than not the unresolved problems of the two peoples-in-flux resulted in friction. Gerchunoff's work, deeply imbued with his Jewish background, and equally permeated by the Argentine milieu, illustrates the predicaments of cohering new communities and imagining novel discourses on the periphery.

Three Versions of Gerchunoff

Since a work is constituted by the history of its reception, the challenges of territory, language, and ideology can best be studied in *The Jewish Gauchos* through three versions of Gerchunoff –the "good," "bad," and "complex." All three begin with the same facts:

Alberto Gerchunoff established an authoritative discursive practice because he founded a new form of Jewish life in a new country. But in order to transform his experiential pioneering into literary pioneering, Gerchunoff had to leave the pampa, move to Buenos Aires, and initiate a successful career as a journalist and writer. It was away from the rural setting he lovingly portrays that he again became a founder. His book was among the earliest Latin American accounts of Jewish emigration to the New World, and among the first works of literary value to be written in modern Spanish by a Jew. Gerchunoff was thus the forerunner of contemporary writers of immigrant stock, the Argentines David Viñas, Andrés Rivera, Alicia Steimberg, Santiago Kovadloff, and Marcos Aguinis, the Mexicans Margo Glantz and Sabina Berman, the Venezuelan Isaac Chocrón, the Brazilians Clarice Lispector and Moacyr Scliar, and a growing number of U.S. Jewish-Latino authors, Marjorie Agosín, Ariel Dorfman, Mario Szichman, Isaac Goldemberg, and Alicia Borinsky. Gerchunoff's existential and literary firstness helped win canonical status for his book.

From this point on, the paths of the three versions fork.

Path I: The Good Gerchunoff, or Argentina, Land of Promise

Territory: Gerchunoff's work rooted Jews on Argentine soil. Bernardo Verbitsky, a fellow intellectual, claimed that Argentine Jews received their citizenship papers through the book, which represented them at their new country's Centennial celebrations. To term a work of fiction a group's "citizenship papers" may be hyperbolic, but it speaks to the power of literature to create what Benedict Anderson calls "imagined communities," in eras of nation-formation.

Gerchunoff understood that during the Centennial, Jews, long bereft of a land, had to declare themselves part and parcel of the community envisioned by Argentina's founders. The most powerful symbol of Argentine territoriality was the gaucho, a figure extoled in speeches, festivities, and books; Leopoldo Lugones's *La guerra gaucha* (1905) [The Gaucho War] and Martiniano Leguizamón's *De cepa criolla* (1908) [Of Native Stock] were just two examples of the copious literature that glorified the pampa cowboy and all things autochthonous. By positioning "Jews" alongside "gauchos," and portraying the immigrants as adopting rural ways, Gerchunoff earned them the right to belong.

Language: Although he knew Yiddish and Russian, the immigrant tongues, testimony after testimony cites Gerchunoff's mastery of the Spanish language, his love for its classical sources, his special devotion for Cervantes. Borges notes Gerchnoff's interest in the twists and turns of vocabulary and syntax (*Figuras* 14). Luis Emilio Soto points to the author's nuanced use of modernist linguistic impressionism (9). Gerchunoff was a champion of *modernismo*, the literary movement that renewed Spanish-language poetry and prose at the start of the century, whose best-known figure was Rubén Darío (see his essay "Rubén Darío"). In *Los gauchos judíos*, Gerchunoff wed modernist chromatism to oral gaucho idioms, and modernist barroquism to archaic Castilian and Judeo-Hispanic turns of phrase, demonstrating that, through their handling of Spanish, Jews could be true Argentines. And if to be true Argentines, Jews had to shed their Old World linguistic heritage, so be it.

Ideology: The Centennial represented the high point of nineteenth-century constitutionalist, free-trade Argentine liberalism. Thanks to this ideology, Argentina had opened its doors to immigration, and Gerchunoff underlined Jewish identification with its tenets, structuring his work like a secular Haggadah, the Passover narration that recounts the Israelites' journey from slavery to freedom. His portrait of the grateful Russo-Jewish immigrants was taken up by the poetic giants of the period, Leopoldo Lugones, in his *Oda a los ganados y a las mieses* [Ode to Flocks and Grains], and Rubén Darío, in *Canto a la Argentina* [Song to Argentina], both written for the Centennial. The implications are evident: Argentina is the modern land of liberty where Jews have been redeemed from Russian oppression. Loss of identity in the assimilationist melting pot was a small price to pay.

This version of the "good" Gerchunoff has become a keystone of official rhetoric, and has given rise to multiple reelaborations, including Juan José Jusid's film *Los gauchos judíos* (1975), and the play by two of Argentina's best-known dramatists, Roberto Cossa and Ricardo Halac, *Aquellos gauchos judíos: recuerdos de la colonia* (1995) [Once Upon a Jewish Gaucho: Memories of the Colony]. Any reference to Argentina's acceptance of Jews, to Jewish integration to the Land of Liberty, inevitably involves an allusion to Gerchunoff's cowboy epic of the new homeland (see also Ricardo Feierstein's anthology, *Los mejores relatos con gauchos judíos*).

Path II: The Bad Gerchunoff, or Argentina, Land of the Disappeared

Territory: Gerchunoff's work misrepresented Jewish rootedness. From the outset, Jews left the colonies for the cities, unable to overcome the pampa's lingering latifundist legacy, crop failures, ICA mismanagment, limited educational opportunities, and rural violence. Gerchunoff himself lived through these bitter experiences; after a drunken gaucho murdered his father, the shattered family moved to Buenos Aires.

In the past two decades younger intellectuals, often victims of repression and exile, took Gerchunoff to task for what they saw as his uncomplicated territorialism. David Viñas, Saúl Sosnowski, Leonardo Senkman, Mario Gerardo Goloboff, and Mario Szichman are among those "parricides on the pampa" who challenged Gerchunoff in critical works and novels, presenting a contradictory deracination or a complex polyterritoriality –Argentina, Europe, Israel– as the more accurate portrait of numerous Argentines, who were scarcely settled on Argentine soil in peace and calm. Bitterly parodying his predecessor, Szichman writes the following in his novel about persecuted Russo-Jewish immigrants sailing to Argentina: "On the first day of the crossing they were shown a film called 'Argentina, the Promised Land.' The screen had been divided into four parts... you could see wheat fields, cows... ships... and a family... looking up at a radiant sun... In the country that had been prepared to fool the immigrants... there were no... short folks... fat folks... or anti-Semites... money grew on trees, and the immigrants became expert broncobusters" (*Los judíos*, 77).

Language: Gerchunoff's skillful handling of Spanish silenced the immigrants' multilingualism and glossed over the impediments to fluency in the new tongue, since then, as now, bilingualism was considered threatening (Senkman, 80-81, 97).

Countering Gerchunoff's perceived strategy of linguistic accomodation, the literary parricides intentionally recreate the difficulties of switching from one linguistic code (Yiddish) to another (Spanish), as in this excerpt from Goloboff: "*Argentineh. Aryentineh. Argentina.* First is the homeland of speech, you must shape a tongue from its very roots. A language that in order to sound like *tug* and mean *día* [day] must be *día* from the deepest depths" (26). Their protagonists incorporate traces of Yiddish to recreate a certain texture of life and to conjure up a storehouse of Jewish experience. Szichman has so many Yiddish words in his novel that he provides a glossary; Feierstein continually interrupts the narrative flow with footnotes to explain *idn, melamed, toit shtibl, schwitzer* (Jews, teacher, death-house, showoff). They foreground bilingual tensions in order to resist homogeneity.

Ideology: Gerchunoff capitulated to the reigning political philosophy for a place in the Argentine sun. In a caustic essay that became the parricides' manifesto, David Viñas forcefully attacks Gerchunoff, to be seconded by Leonardo Senkman (Viñas, "Gerchunoff: gauchos judíos y xenofobia"; Senkman, *La identidad*; see also Lindstrom). Peace and integration, whatever the cost, are the watchwords of *Los gauchos judíos*, Viñas charges. Where, he asks the patriarch, is the conflict, the discontent?

Path III: The Complex Gerchunoff, or Argentina, Land of Contradiction

Which, then, respect or vituperation? Both positions, good and bad, simplify the book, since they are based on the premise that Gerchunoff constructed a one-voiced text and an uncomplicated figure. But did Gerchunoff truly obliterate Jewish ethnic and idiomatic signs? And was his work unremittingly monovocal and accomodationist as claimed? The evidence is more complicated than either side would have it.

Translation is the best way of reading. It forces you to get into the nuts and bolts of the text, to notice the minutae. If criticism looks at macrostructures and makes generalizations, translation focuses on microunits –articles, prepositions, words, phrases. The English translation that forms part of my new look at Gerchunoff, the first ever made of the original 1910 version of *Los gauchos judíos*, uncovers a far greater ideological and linguistic-cultural intricacy than has been allowed, calling for a more nuanced assessment. It has permitted me to rethink the work, and to revise some of my earlier "parricidal" analyses (see "Parricide on the Pampa").

To put it bluntly: most critics base their opinions about what Gerchunoff thought and did in the Centennial period on the wrong text, the *second* version of *Los gauchos judíos* published in 1936, *a quarter of a century after the original*. They make assertions about Gerchunoff's melting-potism and Hispanism unaware –or unconcerned– that they are judging a much later reworking.

Yet the 1910 edition was the Jewish community's entry into the Argentine imagination. It seems imperative to present the foundational text as it was at the founding. At the same time, it is essential not to ignore Gerchunoff's revisions, because they throw light on the depth of his ideological contentiousness and his intense work-in-language right from the book's initial inception. *Los gauchos judíos* must be read in the shuttle space between versions, as a process not as a stasis.

I read the book in just that way, using the insights of genetic criticism and current translation theory. Genetic criticism considers texts to be complex entities constituted of notes, drafts, emendations, and reprintings; translation theory posits interlinguistic transfer as a tense act, meant to lay bare rather than to smooth over roughness and ambiguity[1]. Together, these approaches provide important keys for understanding Gerchunoff's knotty creation. Like Mark Harman's new translation of Kafka's *The Castle*, mine is based on a "restored text," and like Harman's it mimics the strange oscillations and dense counterpoints of the original (xvii).

Three major textual components make up the translation portion of this study: 1) the entire 1910 version of *Los gauchos judíos*, including the barely-known introduction by Martiniano Leguizamón; 2) some significant changes made in 1936, included in brackets (square for omissions,

---

[1] On genetic criticism see Louis Hay and Péter Nagy (eds.) (1982), *Avant-Texte, Texte, Après-Texte*, Paris: Éditions du CNRS, Budapest: Akadémiai Kiadó; and Michael Malicet (ed.) (1986), *Exercices de Critique Génétique* (Cahiers de Textologie), Paris: Minard. I quote from the introduction to *Exercices*: "Toutes ces études illustrent l'importance de la critique génétique qui peut d'autant mieux fournir la base de toute interprétation ultérieure qu'elle révèle la nebuleuse primitive dont nous parlions plus haut, où réside la plupart de temps la source de la polysémie du texte définitif" (4). For current translation theory see, for example, André Lefevre (1992), *Translating Literature: Practice and Theory in a Comparative Literature Context*, New York: Modern Language Association. Also, Suzanne Jill Levine (1991), *The Subversive Scribe: Translating Latin American Literature*, St. Paul: Graywolf.

brace for substitutions); and 3) an appendix containing the two stories added to the second edition. My intent was to give a broad audience a sense of the text and its evolution, not to produce a critical edition with detailed variants[2]. This is the only manner to fully appreciate *Los gauchos judíos* as an experiment in forging a new idiom for a novel experience.

Territory: Rereading *The Jewish Gauchos* as an argumentative, kaleidoscopic work highlights previously-ignored moments –its crucial opening scene, for instance. At a Sabbath gathering set in the Old Country the learned Dayan (rabbinic sage) explicates difficult points in the sacred texts employing the semiotics of talmudic discourse. Traditional Jewish exegesis applied past precedents to present events, and allowed no ideological position to be expressed without a real or hypothetical counterposition (Harshav, 16). Not surprisingly, then, the future immigrants, steeped as they are in the world of the Talmud, critically consider various territorial possibilities, and –just as inevitably– lock horns over the choices.

The antagonists argue contrary points of view: praise for Spain, its mild climate, and kindness to the Jews in centuries gone by; condemnation for blood-saturated Iberia and the horrors of the Inquisition. On the one hand, there is acclaim for Argentina's virtues; but on the other, profound awareness of the millenary pull of Zion, a pull reiterated throughout the work. Even as the newcomers express deep gratitude to the South American refuge, they

---

[2] I have been invited to prepare such an edition for the Colección Archivos, a landmark series of critical editions of twentieth-century Latin American literature funded primarily by UNESCO.

recall that they are not in Jerusalem, that Argentina is not the Promised Land of their ancestors.

Palestine or the Argentine? Benevolent or malevolent new Hispanic earth? Old Russia, where they lived badly but feared God; or the New World, where the young stray from the faith? Gerchunoff does not silence the loud territorial disputations of his time, letting the settlers wrangle and have their say –with the gravity of talmudists, as he frequently points out– signaling to his readers that a single territoriality was far from easy for his persecuted brethren.

Language: Contrary to what might be expected, at the time of the Centennial, when melting-potism and Hispanism were regnant, Gerchunoff's text was exceedingly particularistic and openly yiddishist. The author incorporates the idiosyncratic cultural baggage of the greenhorns: words in Yiddish and Hebrew; multiple footnotes to explain these words; specific references to classic Jewish religious works; translations of Yiddish songs; allusions to popular Yiddish plays and novels; Hebrew-Yiddish forms of biblical names; Spanish calques of Yiddish expressions.

The work brims with non-Spanish expressions: "Cherbale-chaim," "Sana toikef," "Mischnais," "Zeroim,""Gemara", "Iorudea," "ben-yuchid," "shel yod," "umed," "kitol," "Yom Kippur," "Rabbenu Yehudah Ha-Kadosh" (see "Names and Terms" list for meanings). Gerchunoff peppers the stories with allusions to *jerga vulgar* [popular vernacular], a translation of *zhargon*, a common name for Yiddish; to "El canto de la Sulamita," Abraham Goldfaden's famous romantic Yiddish operetta, "Shulamis" (1880); to novels by the best-selling Yiddish author, Shomer; and to the cities of Kishinev, Zhitomir, and Elizabetgrad, important in the history of Eastern European Jewry. Women are addressed Hebraically as "Dvorah" and "Esther," not "Débora" or "Ester," and men as "Rabí," Gerchunoff's rendering of the Yiddish *reb* through multilingual layering that melds Hebrew, Yiddish, and Spanish.

Reb, Yiddish for "mister" (used with the first name), derives from the Hebrew *Rab*, "teacher, rabbi," but it does not have that meaning. *Rabí* does –it is the medieval Spanish term for "rabbi." Gerchunoff's recontextualization of the old Hispanic word appears far from perfect to contemporary eyes, but it gives an idea of the author's linguistic experimentation. I have retained it in my translation to convey the sense of complexity, polyglotism, erudition, archaism, and even estrangement it evokes. *Rabí* exemplifies the tone of Gerchunoff's book, a tone I have endeavored to preserve, since I fully agree with what Mark Harman says about his work on Kafka: "Literary translators must forge a prose style that mimicks the original" (xiv).

To render Gerchunoff's book in breezily colloquial English, to omit its learned circumlocutions and the various strata of language, to substitute the unfamiliar with the familiar, the uncomfortable with the comfortable, would not do it justice. Gerchunoff, it is now clear, was working in uncharted waters and essaying untested solutions. He has not been given enough credit for his efforts even if they now seem eccentric –like *rabí*. Gerchunoff himself often realized where he had gone astray, as can be seen by reading the editions together. What do you call Jewish prayer, the Jewish prayerbook, the holy ark? The author tries on *misa* "mass," *misal* "missal," and *santuario* "a niche for a saint's image." He modifies or eliminates these Christological terms in 1936. But he also omits anti-Christian remarks in the colonists' speech, such as "sus escasas luces de cristiano" 'his thick Christian head,' surely a translation of the Yiddish expression "goyisher kop." In fact, a number of Hebrew-Yiddish idioms are likewise toned down –*kitol* becomes *ropón blanco,* "white tunic," for example, and *Iorudea* merely *los libros* "the books," producing a more generic, though not un-Judaic, second version.

What emerges is hardly a smoothly-blended text in which linguistic wrinkles are quickly ironed out, but an agonistic writing, shaped and reshaped by an author who did not hide the tensions of plurilingualism. (To give another example: Gerchunoff's unadorned *matarife* "slaughterer" for the Yiddish *shochet* may be more grating than a softened rendering like "ritual slaughterer" –but Gerchunoff did not soften the word.) It has not been noted that in Gerchunoff's hands modernist philological cosmopolitanism was not the stuff of fashionable idiomatic borrowings from Paris, or from a long-gone Greco-Latin antiquity; it was an existential struggle. Again and again, the immigrant storyteller registers the greenhorns' tonguetiedness: Spanish, he says, could be as hard as stone.

Ideology: If territory and language are more complicated than has been allowed, then ideology –the crux of the matter– could scarcely be neat. Territory and language are in themselves ideological: Gerchunoff's inscribed the acerbic territorial battles of his day among Zionists, Territorialists, and Socialists; and his verbal toil revealed the strain between the dominant Spanish and the minority Yiddish, the embarrassments of "glottal" assimilation (see Zabus). Gerchunoff's reputation has hinged on the question of assmimilation: Did he, or did he not, produce an accomodationist work, and was this good or bad?

In the rarely-reprinted introduction to the 1910 version, Martiniano Leguizamón lauds the young Jewish immigrant women as the sexualized vessels of cross-ethnic breeding, the genetic crucibles that would smelt down identifiable Jewish traits. But his supposed protégé, Alberto Gerchunoff, gives a far less rosy picture, registering the bitter dismay and profound shame the comely Jewish maidens bring to their families and community when they "blend." This pain remains unaltered in both editions: "It's a disgrace. But is it true? Unfortunately, it is. She ran off with a peon, a gaucho. We saw it coming. She lit the samovar on the Sabbath and ate chickens killed by the peon. What a slut!" Even the gaucho, Gerchunoff's alleged ideal for nativist political correctness, receives ambivalent treatment, sometimes depicted as noble and patriarchal, sometimes as ignoble and murderous.

A gaucho protagonizes the most glaring subversion of the Argentina, Land-of-Technicolor ideology, the narration "Tale of a Stolen Horse," in which he falsely accuses a Jew of filching his mare, as the authorities turn a blind eye. An epigraph from a medieval Castilian document sets the tone: Nuño de Guevara, a Spanish knight, has stolen a fellow hidalgo's sword but has imputed the theft to Don Moisés de Sandobal, "for it is more virtuous to blame the dogs of Jewry than Christian noblemen." The learned slaughterer talmudically teases out the reluctant message: the landscape and the peasants may change but a Jew is a Jew; Argentina may be not so different from Russia, after all.

Gerchunoff attempts to end on a high note –"I want to believe that it won't always be this way"– yet leaves the disturbing implications. These are only underscored by "The Silver Candelabra," one of the two stories he added in 1936. This fiction about the theft from a Jewish home of the valuable and symbolic object –Will Judaism be "stolen" in Argentina? How safe are Jews in the Argentine haven?– closes that most familiar edition of Gerchunoff's paean. He was uncannily prescient: in 1994, a bomb destroyed the institutional home of Argentine Jewry, the AMIA building on Pasteur Street which housed an irreplaceable library of Jewish authors –including Gerchunoff (see Aizenberg 1994).

Republishing the book in 1936, some twenty-five years after its initial appearance, was itself a symptom of the artistic and ideological restlessness I have been tracing. On the one hand, it vigorously affirmed Jewish identity at a time of growing anti-Semitism in Europe and Argentina; on the other, it reflected Gerchunoff's distancing from the colonies' original ethos and speech milieu, and from the greater hopefulness of the earlier period (see also Senkman 1999). That does not mean that we can neatly posit a first, Hebraic, unbeat version and a second, dehebraized, downbeat writing, since the quarrelsomeness and questioning are there from the start. Read against the long-accepted grain, Don Alberto emerges less as the high priest of quietism –the object of "parricide on the pampa"– and more as a dynamic forerunner of intellectuals who today strive with homogeneizing ideologies, problematic postmodernities, and impoverishing ethnic, linguistic, and historical verities.

BIBLIOGRAPHY

Aizenberg, Edna (1987), "Parricide on the Pampa: Deconstructing Gerchunoff and His Jewish Gauchos", in: *Folio* 17: 24-39.
———. (1994), "Alongside the Dead in Argentina", in: *The New York Times*, Op-Ed, 7 August.
———. (1997), "Postmodern or Post-Auschwitz: Borges and the Limits of Representation", in: *Variaciones Borges* 3: 141-152.
Borges, Jorge Luis, "Borges conversa sobre Gerchunoff", in: *Figuras de nuestro tiempo*: 11-16.
Cossa, Roberto, and Ricardo Halac (1995), *Aquellos gauchos judíos: recuerdos de la colonia*, Buenos Aires: AMIA.
Feierstein, Ricardo (1994), *Mestizo*, Buenos Aires: Planeta
———.(1998), *Los mejores relatos con gauchos judíos: De Alberto Gerchunoff a Marcos Aguinis*, Buenos Aires: Ameghino.
Foster, David William (1994), *Cultural Diversity in Latin American Literature*, Albuquerque: University of New Mexico Press.
Gerchunoff, Alberto (1910), *Los gauchos judíos*. Prólogo de Martiniano Leguizamón, La Plata: Joaquín Sésé.
———. (1936), *Los gauchos judíos*. Prólogo de Martiniano Leguizamón. Nueva edición corregida y aumentada, Buenos Aires: Gleizer.
———. (1979), *Figuras de nuestro tiempo*, Buenos Aires: Vernácula.
Goloboff, Mario Gerardo (1976), *Caballos por el fondo de los ojos*, Barcelona: Planeta.
Harman, Mark (1998), "Translator's Preface", in: Franz Kafka, *The Castle*, New York: Schocken: XIII-XXIII.
Harshav, Benjamin (1993), *Language in the Time of Revolution*, Berkeley: University of California Press.
Hay, Louis, and Nagy, Péter (eds.) (1982), *Avant-Texte, Texte, Après-Texte*, Paris: Éditions du CNRS, Budapest: Akadémiai Kiadó.

Lefevre, André (1992), *Translating Literature: Practice and Theory in a Comparative Literature Context*, New York: Modern Language Association.

Levine, Suzanne Jill (1991), *The Subversive Scribe: Translating Latin American Literature*, St. Paul: Graywolf.

Liacho, Lázaro (1975), *Alberto Gerchunoff*, Buenos Aires: Colombo.   ·

Lindstrom, Naomi (1989), *Jewish Issues in Argentine Literature*, Columbia: University of Missouri Press.

Malicet, Michael (ed.) (1986), *Exercices de Critique Génétique* (Cahiers de Textologie), Paris: Minard.

Senkman, Leonardo (1983), *La identidad judía en la literatura argentina*, Buenos Aires: Pardes.

———. (1999), "Los gauchos judíos: una lectura desde Israel", in: *Estudios Interdisciplinarios de América Latina y el Caribe* 10/1:141-152.

Soto, Luis Emilio (1964), "Alberto Gerchunoff: labrador y boyero". Intro. to *Los gauchos judíos*, Buenos Aires: EUDEBA: 5-14.

Szichman, Mario (1971), *Los judíos del mar dulce*, Buenos Aires; Caracas: Galerna-Síntesis 2000.

Viñas, David (1975), "Gerchunoff: gauchos judíos y xenofobia", in: *Literatura argentina y realidad política: apogeo de la oligarquía*, Buenos Aires: Siglo Veinte.

Zabus, Chantal (1991), *The African Palimpsest*, Amsterdam-Atlanta: Rodopi

FOREWORD

I found this book waiting for me at a most propitious time. I had just come back from the country where I spent many a quiet afternoon in the fresh pampa air; I was still imbued with the spirit of the plains, and the image of the sunsets that turn the green hills into a fiery red was fresh in my mind. This new book, so full of Argentine flavor and aroma, revived these fond memories of my native region. I enjoyed it immensely, since I am an unabashed enthusiast of works deeply rooted in our tradition.

This book, then, brought back warm remembrances of a region whose landscapes and sensations are closely bound to the best years of my childhood. A writer who was not born under these benevolent skies, but who grew to love and to understand them, has offered me a bouquet from my native land. Just a few short years of contact with the land and its original inhabitants were enough for him to ably capture its spirit and unforgettable images in colorful sketches of the Jewish colonies established near Montiel. The colonists cut their first furrows at the edge of this wild and impenetrable forest, long ago a refuge for men whose savage acts of bravery became the stuff of legend.

Gerchunoff's stories are short, yet the author succeeds admirably in describing the countryside and its folk. The book rings true, and it is filled with so much local color. The episodes first seem scattered and unrelated, but they gradually come together through the strong expressions of love for the land and of gratitude for its bounty. In Gerchunoff's small colony of Rachil we meet the classic, sharp-nosed bearded old Jews and their sad and wrinkled wives, as well as graceful young Jewish maidens bronzed by the radiant sun. There are dark-haired girls with deep, mysterious gazes, and golden-haired lasses with thick long braids, eyes as blue as the Virgin's, and shapely bodies whose sculptural forms are revealed whenever the pampa rain drenches their rustic cotton dresses...

The author loves these women with brotherly affection. He portrays them with great tenderness because they remind him of the biblical shepherd girls who grazed their gentle flocks in green pastures. He is moved to poetry when he recalls the august women of Scripture, and he moves the reader as well. Raquel, Rebecca, Esther, Miriam, and Ruth so captivate us with their strong and simple beauty that we forgive them for the ease with which they violate the strict prohibition against falling in love with men who are not of their race, and lose their hearts to the gallant gauchos who woo them with love songs and plaintive guitars, or with displays of horsemanship.

These young women play an important role in the book. They are the crucible of love that is forging a handsome and manly new figure: the Jewish gaucho. The aged, bearded rabbis may continue to chant hoary lamentations –their prayers will be in vain. Their children no longer frequent the synagogue; they are abandoning the traditional ways and adopting local customs and dress. Under the influence of their surroundings they are developing the sense of freedom and the spirit of courage characteristic of our country people.

The author describes how the young Jews of Rachil rope, lasso and saddle their horses in criollo style. We see the quick-witted Jacobo wheeling a frisky stallion, dressed like a gaucho with a knife tucked into his silver-studded belt, and lead boleadoras to pummel the animal's back. He is the colony's first true Argentine, who prefers the taste of bitter mate to that of tea brewed in the samovar brought over from the far-off Russian village. And as the mate is passed from hand to hand around the fire, Favel Duglach, the wandering bard, spins his yarns, mingling stories about the exile in Babylon with the tale of the gaucho who knifes a tiger deep in the wilds of Montiel.

The process will be slow but sure: the old Jews will disappear, and their ancient biblical longings will be buried with them. Through the fusion of bloods, their children's children will become Argentines free of worry and travail, bursting with affection for the fertile land, thankful to the peaceful, joyous homeland. The culmination of this process will be celebrated on the second centennial of Argentine independence, when the immigrants' grandchildren will sing glorious hymns to their country's liberty.

In *The Jewish Gauchos* the young writer gives us a wonderful glimpse of rural life at a time when it is undergoing change. His vignettes will surely be useful to future students of one of the most curious aspects of this transformation. By choosing a local theme the author has earned a place of honor among the thinning ranks of national authors. He should serve as an example to native-born writers who reject the countryside as a source of inspiration and who instead churn out sterile and imitative exotica devoid of feeling or originality.

The arrival of Jewish colonists on the plains once dominated by outlaws and free-riding gauchos gave the author the opportunity to depict both the native Argentines and the immigrant Jews, whose customs, language, and dress were foreign to the pampa. In these

sensitive little sketches –much like miniature watercol-
ors– we see the venerable figure of the rabbi next to that
of the aged herdsman Don Remigio, who, faithful to the
cult of courage that was the hallmark of the gaucho of
old, stabs his own son in the head rather than face the
shame of the young man's cowardice in a fight.

Don Remigio comes alive through Gerchunoff's skillful portrayal. We sense that the author must have spent
many a night around Don Remigio's fire listening to his
tales of sorrow and glory as a lancer in Urquiza's armies;
tales told without pompous exaggeration, with the sim-
plicity typical of our country folk. Perhaps Don Remigio
was his first teacher in the art of pampa life –and what a
teacher! He taught the young boy how to do the hard
work of a gaucho, and with his slow, deliberate speech
and colorful turns of phrase, he instilled in his student a
love for the landscape and the sheltering sky of Entre
Ríos. Gerchunoff transmits these feelings to us when he
has Rabí Abraham sing the praises of that sky on a clear,
moonlit night made for blissful reverie.

The finest pages of the book are without a doubt those
devoted to nature. Gerchunoff exercises great artistic con-
trol in his suggestive vignettes –perhaps too much con-
trol. They would have been more effective had he written
with less restraint, with larger doses of local color.
Indeed, at those moments when the evocations succeed in
breaking out of their narrow confines, they come alive
and vibrate with emotion. If the author plans to suprise
us with more such fine writing in his forthcoming novel
of manners, *Land of Zion*, then we can hail the publication
of his short sketches as an auspicious beginning.

With this work of art and truth, Alberto Gerchunoff
has proven his undying affection for his adoptive country, an affection that will surely grow when he holds the

first child born on Argentine soil in his arms. He has also revealed the sensibility of a poet who knows how to transmit his deep feeling for our natural world with the kind of intensity that we find in Joaquín González's or Fray Mocho's paeans to the countryside.

We happily salute him as one of the writers of the land. He has a special gift for finding hidden beauty in the familiar and the mundane; he possesses great powers of observation and a keen eye for capturing the restrained emotions and peaceful tempo of country life.

I hope that he continues to explore this rich vein, unencumbered by ethnic considerations or literary canons. He should find his own rhythm, allowing the images to flow from his pen unbridled, like a spirited horse let loose on the pampa of my beloved Entre Ríos, galloping beneath the sun and the moon, with a song of love on his lips and a zest for life in his heart...

My warmest greetings to his delicious Jewish maidens, whose steps I followed throughout the book as they turned young men's fancies away from the local girls, while their elders intoned ancient benedictions for the bountiful land of golden grain in their archaic tongue. I likewise salute the old gauchos –remnant of a vanquished race–, whose legendary tales awaken nostalgic feelings of love and respect in children's hearts.

Martiniano Leguizamón

> With an outstretched arm the Lord
> delivered us from Pharaoh, in Egypt.
>
> *The Passover prayers*

Behold my brethren from the cities and the colonies, the republic is celebrating its great feast, the paschal feast of its liberation.

Bright are the days and sweet the nights; hymns rise up to departed heroes; voices of jubilation reach the skies, hued blue and white like our flag. Meadows come alive with flowers, fields with green.

Remember how, back in Russia, ye set tables to celebrate the ritual of the Passover? This is a greater Passover.

Rest your plows and deck your tables. Cover them with cloths of white. Sacrifice your choisest kids, set out the wine and salt of benediction. Generous is the flag that succors the ancient hurts of our race, that binds its wounds with maternal care. Wandering Jews, tortured and torn, redeemed captives, let us bend the knee beneath the unfurled banner; in unison, beside choirs bejeweled by light, let us intone the song of songs that begins thus: "Hear Oh ye mortals..."

Buenos Aires, May of the Argentine
Centennial

ICA map of its settlements in South America

GENESIS

Blessed art Thou, only King of all nations,
for the fruit of the earth and the trees.

The daily benedictions

The strongest, most illustrious men of
Judaea tilled the soil; when the Chosen
People went into captivity they worked at
dangerous and lowly trades, and lost
God's favor.

Mischnais, Zeroim, First Order,
Tractate on Agriculture

In the sordid, snow-covered city of Tulchin, a city of glorious rabbis and hoary synagogues, the news of America
filled the Jews' hearts with dreams. Whenever some visit-
ing rabbi preached in the temple, whenever some dis-
patch in a newspaper from Odessa spoke about the far-off
lands of the New World, the Jews would congregate in
the home of their most important coreligionist and ponder the plans for emigration with the graveness of talmudists.

I remember those gatherings well. Those were the
days when restrictive edicts multiplied in the Holy
Russian Empire. Cossack lances were destroying ancient
synagogues; old arks (*santuarios*), solemn, noble, historic
arks, their tops graced by the shining double triangle of
Solomon, were carted through the streets. I remember
the rabbis' words and the women's weeping when the
Cossacks burned the holy books in the great synagogue,

the synagogue donated to the city by my grandparents. The entire community dressed in black. It was the eve of Shavuos, but the palm fronds for the spring festival were covered in mourning; the women and children were covered in mourning, and the old men fasted forty days and forty nights. It was then that Rabbi Yehudah Anakroi, the Dayan, traveled to Paris to reach an agreement with the Baron Hirsch about the founding of Jewish colonies in Argentina. When he returned, the Jews gathered in our home to hear the aged Doctor of the Law bring the good tidings:

"Baron Hirsch, may God bless him, has promised to save us. My colleague, Rabbi Zadock Kahn, will guide his efforts."

The Dayan went on to paint a wonderful future for his persecuted people, with an eloquence honed in synagogue debates. His emotion-filled voice trembled, as when he preached in the temple about the Promised Land. His hand, dry and gnarled from turning the pages of the texts, stroked his long white beard. His small, lively eyes sparkled, illuminated by the light of prophecy.

"You'll see, my brethren, you'll see!" he said. "It's a land where everyone works and where the Christians won't hate us because there the sky is different, and justice and mercy fill their hearts."

Rabbi Yehudah Ankroi's words soothed the dejected spirits of the sad Jews, who looked like phantoms by the light of the moon shining thorough the tall windows. Lost in extasy, they managed to mumble,

"Amen."

* * *

On Saturday afternoons Tulchin's most respected citizens gathered in my parents' house to engage in religious discussions. The Dayan would clarify difficult points with precedents culled from celebrated polemics held in Spain. He was well versed in Talmudic wisdom, in homiletic folklore, and in the occult doctrines of the Kabbalah. His discourses in that intimate setting sounded like the sermons recorded in the thick volumes –written in the archaic language of the Hassidim– that he kept on his bookshelves, richly carved from Jerusalem wood.

On one occasion the rabbi from Tolna sang the praises of Spain. He extoled its mild climate and recalled the era when the people of Israel lived on Spanish soil.

"Spain would be the most desireable land for us," he said with a sigh, "were it not for the curse of the synagogue that weighs upon it."

The Dayan reacted angrily:

"Machshemom izichrom!" he exclaimed in Hebrew. "May it perish and turn to dust! I have never been able to mention the name of Spain without blood welling up in my eyes and hate filling my heart. May God, in His justice, turn it into an everlasting pyre for having tortured our brethren and burned our priests. In Spain, Jews stopped tilling the earth and shepherding their flocks. Do not forget, my dear rabbi, what it says in Zeroim, the first book of the Mischnais, about life on the land: It alone is wholesome and worthy of God's grace. That's why, when Rabbi Zadock Kahn informed me about the immigration to Argentina, I forgot the return to Zion in the midst of my joy, and remembered the words of Yehudah Halevi: Zion is wherever peace and happiness reign. We'll all go to Argentina, and go back to working the land and shepherding our flocks, which the Most High will bless. Remember the words of Zeroim, the first book of the Mishnais: Only those who live of their flocks and their harvests are pure of heart and worthy of eternal Paradise. If we go back to that way of life we will be returning to our original path. May I live to kiss the earth of the new land, and to bless my children's children under its skies."

Thus spoke Rabbi Yehudah Anakroi, my father's venerable friend, last representative of those great rabbis whose wisdom brought brilliance to the synagogues of Portugal and Spain. As I repeat his words, I kiss the earth of the new land of peace and happiness in his name; and like those Jews who heard him speak, I say,

"Amen."

Cutting the furrow

THE FURROW

A cold wind is blowing through the distant maguey trees. The countryside glistens beneath a thick, snow-white frost, and the morning lingers lazily, sprawled under a fine, sun-dimming fog. Up ahead, farmers are already fast at work; whenever the wind slows you can hear their plow's turning wheel.

We need to mark off a new plot for tilling. We have yoked the gentlest oxen, and set a stake tied with a little red cloth at five hundred meters. We will cut two furrows, one coming, the other going. We all realize what a solemn occasion this is.

The pair of oxen stands ready, rythmically chewing its cud, as if also aware of the day's special meaning. But it is Barbos, the dog, who really understands what is happening. The morning is too interesting for the rest of the family to stay indoors. Here then comes Mother with a jug of steaming hot coffee, followed by the girls. Little by little, everything is set.

"Are we ready?"

"Ready!"

My brother steadies the plow as I guide the oxen. "Right! Left!" The oxen understand the importance of their mission, so they walk slowly, with a dignified gait. The stake faces a chain tied to the middle of the yoke, a solid yoke fashioned by hand from quebracho wood on those days when rain kept us from working in the fields.

The plow groans. Mother and the girls are marching behind it, keeping its slow pace, while the sparrow flitters about, less serious than Barbos, who runs ahead of the oxen, mimicking their step by moving his head back and forth and wagging his tail. Barbos has the easy humor and keen intelligence of an experienced farmer, so he has no trouble understanding why this is a momentous event. He walks on, ignoring the frequent partidges and bothersome sparrows. The oxen pull the plow forward, sweet and resigned, foaming at the mouth, yet scarcely feeling the weight of the yoke ignominiously strapped to their enormous horns. And the earth, chilled by winter, yields, sending forth a strong, moist aroma that the family breaths in like deep perfume, as the plow's wheel chants the psalm of bountiful harvests.

Off in the distance, the little cloth unfurls, proud as a standard, and a sparrow gives chase to a snake lolling in the sun.

FRESH MILK

The girl sat by the fence, milking the gentle cow. The sweet animal stood still as her calf nibbled at the tiny blades of grass. Moist drops of dew melted in its mouth like crystal beads perched on a bed of red. Flashes of pink crisscrossed the horizon; the colony was waking up. Gates opened and bearded elders appeared in doorways, mumbling their morning prayers. Dawn –God's divine dawn praised by holy rabbis– brought the day's first exchanges:

"Remigio, should we rake today?"

"No, Don Ephraim. There's been too much rain. We'd better plow."

"All right. Come in and have some mate. Listen, Remigio, yoke up Chico and Feo."

The sound of voices carried on the early morning breeze wafted over from the nearby house:

"Rabí Ephraim, are you going over to the station?"

"I'm sending my farmhand."

"Then have him ask if there's any mail for me."

And down by the picket fence, its poles twisted like wizened carob pods, the girl is milking the gentle cow. She bends, and as her fingers squeeze the magnificent udders they let forth a stream of foam. In the soft light of the autumn dawn the girl's full, firm breasts shine through her parted blouse like fruit ripened by a summer sun.

Drop by drop, with a soft music that keeps time with the girl's breathing and the cow's quiet snorting, the milk fills the pail.

Dark waves of hair fall over her shoulders as she works, and her peasant garb sheaths the luscious fullness of a body punctuated by generous hips, displaying the rythmic lines of a rustic clay amphora. The clear light of dawn accentuates her eyes –eyes as blue as the Holy Virgin's–, and her upturned nose captures all of her race's innate charms.

Gentle tiller of the soil! As I behold you I recall the august women of Scripture. Amidst the fields' pastoral calm you bring to life those biblical heroines who shepherded sweet flocks on the hills of Judaea, who raised their voices in Temple courtyards to sing festive hymns to Jehovah. Raquel, you are Esther, Rebecca, Dvorah, or Judith. You revive their labors under a sheltering sky, as your hands bind blond sheaves shimmering in a sea of golden wheat toasted by the fiery sun; a sea of wheat planted by your brothers and blessed by the patriarchal hand of a father no longer a moneylender or a martyr in Bessarabia.

Raquel, you renew Jerusalem's days of old, with the gentle cow and meek lamb at your side. See how the hills come alive with joyous labor, how the brook sings the morning's praises and renders its offering of fresh water to the horse and the ox. And as in the Jerusalem of bygone eras, your father, his brow covered by the small black leather box containing verses from Scripture, prays to the God of Israel, Lord of Hosts, master of light, air, and earth. He prays to Him with the ancient Hebrew words:

"Baruch ata Adonai..."

Rain

The afternoon is fading into sweet, peaceful nightfall; flashes of yellow crisscross the blackening sky. The animals, sensing the hour, slowly make their way back to the corral. Work has ended; dark ushers in a restful calm. Behind the houses, plows stand idle, like mute lyres, and the mare's bell tinkles by the brook.

Old men begin to intone the evening prayers as a father inquires:

"Is Juan back yet?"

"No, he's gone get the saddle he left at the butcher's the other day."

"What about Rebecca?"

"She's washing her hair."

"Is La Rosilla all right?"

"Yes, she's tied up in the corral."

Amidst the deepening shadows, Rosilla the cow nods her head in melancholy assent.

Suddenly, the sky bursts open, shattering the waning sunlight into a thousand bright diamonds refracted in the luminous raindrops.

Someone shouts out:

"What about the calf?"

Rebecca rushes out and grabs the calf before it can attach itself to the mother's rich udders. She runs out half-dressed, oblivious to the rain that is furiously drenching her finely-formed breasts. She runs out barely covered by a towel, looking majestic as a strong, rustic goddess shining under the crowning glory of her dark, flowing mane.

SIESTA

Sabbath Day: holy day of rest sanctified by rabbinic writings, extoled in Yehudah Halevi's poetic hymns. The colony is dozing lazily, heavy with sleep. Its whitewashed little houses, thatched in yellow, sparkle in the sun, the benign sun of a country spring. A solemn peace has descended from a sky cleansed by last evening's shower, and sweet murmurs rise up from the earth. Orchards are abloom, fields alive with green. In the center of the pasture a brook is intoning its georgic melody, the slow, grave chant of water spinning in small eddies. Up on the road, a dead snake lies motionless like a scribble in the dust.

The flocks are resting in the pasture. The oxen chew their cud and shake their heads, as if in thought; their horns shatter the sunlight into a thousand streaks of blue. This is also their holy day. Over in a corner the mare's bell is tinkling and her colt is cavorting happily in the grass.

The slaughterer's house lies in silence. Rabí Abraham is asleep, and so are his sons; there are still hours to go before the afternoon prayer. Jacobo, the orphaned farmhand, is busy braiding his pony's tail. A light wind ruffles his bombachas and the sunlight glistens on his boleadoras and knife. The old grandmother is sitting by the door, holding her granddaughter on her lap. She wears a milk-white kerchief on her white hair; her wrinkled, sun-browned face bears the marks of deep suffering. She sighs heavily as the little girl begins to hum a tune.

"Jacobo, leave that pony alone! It's the Sabbath."

"Am I working, Doña Raquel?"

"Yes, my child, you are. Hasn't Abraham taught you that you have to rest on the Sabbath?"

In the background, the little girl is softly singing her melody [in the popular vernacular]:

Weep and lament, Oh ye daughters of Zion,
Weep and lament with us...

"Grandma, do you know that song? I've never heard you sing it."

"Yes, my child, I know it. Let's see now, your hair is good and filthy."

"I just had it washed yesterday."

"It's still dirty."

Slowly and patiently, the grandmother runs her fingers through the child's hair.

"You see," she says, clicking her fingernails, "here's one... no, two, three, four... You have so many..."

"Grandma, tell me that story about Kishinev," the child says, still humming her tune.

"Here's another one! They've done a very bad job on you, my dear."

"And the ballad about the shepherd, Grandma?"

"That's a nice one, my love. Did you learn it?"

"Rebecca taught it to me."

The grandmother cleans and cleans the blond curls, as her granddaughter sings on:

There was once a little shepherd in Canaan.
[When he became rich he traded in grain.]

"Grandma, tell me the story about Kishinev. Do you remember it?"

"Yes, child. See, I've just found one more. I'm telling

you, they didn't wash out your hair properly. It's full of lice: one two, three. Look at this huge one! They'd eat you alive if I weren´t be cleaning them out."

"But doesn't the Book say that you shouldn't kill living things?

["What are living things called?"

"Cherba-le-chaim."]

"Yes, my child."

"Well then..."

"Cows are living beings and your father still slaughters them."

Just then, a neighbor, Don Zacarías, stops by to greet them.

"Good Sabbath, Doña Raquel."

"Good year, Rabí Zacarías. Here I am with my granddaughter. They've done a very poor job on her hair."

"We have to take good care of our children, don't we, Doña Raquel. What would become of them if we didn't?"

"May God watch over us, Rabí Zacarías. Children love their parents only when they're gone."

"That's true. You know what the Commentator says: Children miss their parents when they die just as the plucked flower misses its stem... Hey, Jacobo, don't you know that it's the Sabbath?"

"I'm not plowing, Don Zacarías. I'm just grooming my horse. I've already given him water and now I'm getting him ready to round up the flock after dark."

"Your're not supposed to be cleaning him either."

"Isn't Doña Raquel cleaning Miriam's head?"

"Leave that gaucho alone! All he knows is how to be fresh. Look at him! He even looks like a gaucho in that getup –bombachas, belt, knife, and even those horrible little lead things to kill partridges! But when he's in synagogue he keeps his mouth shut because he doesn't know his prayers. And to think that he's been educated by my son, the slaughterer!"

"That's how the young are nowadays. By the way, have you heard the news?"

"What news? Tell me."

Don Zacarías nodded towards Ishmael Ruderman's rundown hut.

"Well, his daughter..."

"Yes, I know. Abraham's already told me. What a terrible shame. But is it really true?"

"I'm afraid it is. This morning Rabí Ishmael didn't come to the synagogue, and it was his turn to read today's chapter. Then my brother told us what had happened. She ran off with his hired hand. Would you believe it? With a gaucho!"

Jacobo interrupted their conversation.

"Remigio's a terrific fellow. He taught me how to lasso and how to break in a horse."

"You see what I mean?" Doña Raquel exclaimed. "It's all the same to this little renegade... It's as if she ran off with a Jew."

The sun begins to set, and the herdsman's voice sounds off in the distance. Rabí Abraham appears in the doorway, covering his imposing figure with the "little tunic," whose four ritual fringes brush against Raquel's hair.

"Good Sabbath, Rabí Abraham."

"Good Sabbath, good year, Rabí Zacarías. What do you say to the news?"

"We saw it coming. She always lit the samovar on the Sabbath and ate chickens slaughtered by the gaucho. What a slut! Do you think there are enough people in the synagogue to hold the service?"

Rebecca comes out with her hair tousled from sleep. She sits down under the eave where the tools are kept, and greets everyone in a husky voice. Jacobo, now bored with the horse, is sharpening his knife on the corral's wire fence. When he hears Rebecca, he starts to sing Remigio's tune:

Girl of my thoughts,
Vidalitá...

Gateway, synagogue

NEW IMMIGRANTS

There were some two hundred families gathered in the Domínguez station that morning. A group of new immigrants was due to arrive on the ten o'clock train to settle in an area not far from San Gregorio, near the thickets where according to local legend outlaws and tigers had their lairs.

It was a fragrant spring morning; fields of daisies dotted the joyously green countryside.

The general store was packed with people talking excitedly about the immigrants coming from Russia, among whom, rumor had it, there was a rabbi from Odessa. According to the information we had, the venerable talmudist from the Yeshivah of Vilna had been to Paris where he was cordially received by Baron Hirsch, the "Grandfather of the Colonies."

While we waited, the stationmaster chatted with the sergeant, who had come from Villaguay to help with the new arrivals, and some gauchos played a game of taba, surrounded by curious onlookers.

Our colony's slaughterer spent the time arguing with his counterpart from Rosh Pinah, hoping to better his adversary and to impress the large crowd with his infinite wisdom. The two began talking about the rabbi who was expected. The slaughterer from Rosh Pinah knew him from Vilna, where they had studied the holy books together. The sage was a kind man, he said, well-versed in Talmud. He had participated in an expedition to buy land in Palestine before Grandfather Hirsch began his project.

"He's never practiced the rabbinate," the visitor from Rosh Pinah informed the colonists who were listening in on the conversation. "After finishing his studies he went into business in Odessa and wrote articles in *Hatzphira*, a newspaper published in ancient Hebrew."

The two men went on to argue over a fine point of domestic law, and the slaughterer from Rachil cited the decision of the great Ramboam[1] concerning the killing of cattle.

The wait for the newcomers awakened dormant memories. Everyone in the crowd relived the morning of departure from the Czar's cruel empire and the day of arrival in the promised land, in the Jerusalem extoled in sermons and acclaimed in leaflets whose Russian verses, printed under the portrait of Baron Hirsch, praised the excellence of the soil:

To Palestine and to the Argentine,
We'll go, to sow,
We'll go, brothers and friends,
To live and be free...

"Don Abraham," the sergeant called out, "here comes the train."

A murmur of excitement ran through the crowd. A cloud of smoke could be seen rising beyond the hill, curling up into the clear sky. As the train drew near, everyone broke out in cheers.

The immigrants began to pour out of the cars. They looked sick and miserable, but hope shone in their eyes.

---

[1] Ramboam: Maimonides. Ramboam is a contraction of Rabbenu Moisés ben Maimon, the sage's given name *(author's note)*.

The rabbi was the last one to come down. He was a tall, stocky man with a jovial face covered by a thick white beard. The colonists surrounded him and began to shower him with words of welcome.

Don Abraham quickly placed himself at the rabbi's side; the weary travelers trudged along, carrying their children and their bundles, overwhelmed by the beauty of the deep blue morning.

They stopped at the general store, where Don Abraham, standing on top of a tree trunk, greeted them with high-blown Hebrew phrases. The rabbi replied in the name of the immigrants, opening with a verse from Isaiah, and going on to report the frightening news from Russia.

"But here," he declared, "we will work our land, shepherd our flocks, and earn our bread."

Then, swelling with enthusiasm, looking as imposing as a prophet with his beard unfurling like a banner in the wind, he jumped off the trunk, hugged the sergeant, and planted a kiss on his mouth.

The long caravan picked up its slow march under the warm splendor of the morning sun.

In the fields

THRESHING

The farmhands finished loading our sacks of wheat at nine. The threshing machine stopped turning, and we gathered for our morning coffee by the shade of the tall, unthreshed bundles. A fierce sun beat down on us. The cropped fields shimmered in the strong light like the bristles of giant golden brush.

Far off, in the pasture, in the gullies, in the grassy knolls by the small lagoons, the oxen were grazing, slow and sad, blissfully oblivious to the lapwings' boisterous cackling.

The mayor, an astute and loquacious old man who had been elected by the settlers at an assembly in the synagogue, was marveling at the harvest and the quality of the wheat.

He was practically illiterate, and his knowlege of Scripture was limited to a few select passages committed to memory that he recited on the appropriate occasions –when he distributed a piece of fencing, or supervised the purchase of a roll of wire.

On this particular hot and sunny morning, standing in the shade of the bundles, and surrounded by his fellow farmers, he began to sound forth about the wonders of country life.

"I am well aware that we are not in Jerusalem," he commenced. "I am well aware that this is not the land of our ancestors. But here we can sow and harvest our grain, and at night, when we come in from the threshing floor, we can thank the Almighty for having brought us out of Russia, where we were hated and lived in misery and fear."

"The wheat in Bessarabia was much whiter," the slaughterer retorted. "Besides, in Russia we lived badly, but we feared God and followed His Law. Here, the young people are turning into gauchos."

A sharp whistle from the machine broke up the gathering. It was Moisés Hintler's turn to have his wheat threshed. Hintler, a short, thin man, stood quietly beside the revolving drum, his small, round, myopic eyes brimming with happiness. His wife, prematurely aged by the miseries suffered in her native village, stood near him, while their daughter Dvorah, a lively and robust young woman, prepared the family's lunch.

The work began. We climbed up to the top of the pile of grain to get at the highest sheaves, while the workers oiled and prepared the huge machine.

"Say, Moisés," the mayor shouted. "Did you have such piles of wheat in Vilna? Or were you just a miserable little jeweler who eeked out a few rubles a month fixing old watches? Now you have your own field, and your own wheat and cows."

He raised a glass of rum, and toasted:

"As we used to say in Russia: May your land always be so fertile that you can't harvest its entire crop!"

Moisés did not react. He continued to stand mutely beside the machine, his head swimming with half-buried memories of his pitiful existence in Vilna, of his bitter, dismal life as a Jew.

The large drum of the thresher began to turn, and grain came spilling out like a shower of pearly raindrops falling from the sunny sky, like a stream of golden water descending from the biblically-blessed firmament. Moisés extended his hand, and let his fingers luxuriate in the cascade of yellow wheat.

"Take a look, my dear ones," he finally murmured to his

wife and daughter. "Take a good look. This wheat is ours."

And as he spoke, two large teardrops ran down his cheeks, furrowed by the wages of misery. They slowly blended with the grains pouring into the first sack of his wheat harvest.

By the harvesting machine

THE DESTROYED ORCHARD

It was a clear, warm day. A soft wind was blowing gently through the freshly-planted fields of green that stretched out on both sides of the village. The boys were herding the cattle into the large clearing that separated the two rows of houses, preparing to take them to pasture.

We were enjoying the period of rest just before the start of a new planting season, so that morning we had time to go to the synagogue. It was the anniversary of a neighbor's death, and his sons had to recite the memorial prayers.

The main topic of conversation was last night's altercation between two feuding families. The mayor had made valiant efforts to broker a peace, ably assisted by the learned slaughterer, who, well-versed in the requisite legal precedents, cited salomonic arguments and mouthed edifying quotes. After each side had hurled a sufficient number of insults at the other, and had dredged up enough damaging gossip about the rival family, a reconciliation was effected.

Each of the former enemies now felt free to give us errands to run at the station, where we had decided to spend the afternoon.

"Pick up my mail, won't you?"

"Bring me the rice I bought last Sunday."

By the time we left the synagogue, the sky had turned a deep blue, and it seemed to hang lower. The orchards stood out in full bloom behind the houses, some whitewashed, others thatched in yellow. There were very few trees dotting the landscape, but right in front of our house a large paradise tree solemnly shaded a portion of the road.

When we were close to home we noticed the dim outlines of a cloud on the red horizon, far, far off in the distance.

"It looks like rain," someone remarked.

"It sure does," the farmhand agreed.

Around eleven the cloud began to grow bigger; it now covered large patches of sky.

"Go and ask Don Gabino what he thinks," the mayor suggested.

But Don Gabino, the colony's herdsman, was out pasturing the animals. The old gaucho, who always boasted that he had once fought under the great Crispín Velázquez, served as our local skywatcher, and his forecasts were never wrong.

A sense of unease settled over the farmers as they dispersed for lunch. The cloud was growing larger and more menacing. It seemed to be expanding and moving closer to the ground at the same time.

People were accustomed to bad weather, but the sight of this strange cloud coming on without strong winds or thunder frightened them. They leaned on their fences with their eyes anxiously glued to the sky, transfixed by the strange phenomenon. We forgot about our trip to the station, about the reconciliation effected by the slaughterer after the two orphans had completed the memorial prayers for their dead father.

We just stood there, staring at the now-monstrous mass that was covering the sky and slowly moving toward us. Within a short hour the mass came alive, and a sea of locust descended on everything in sight.

"It's the plague!" the slaughterer shouted.

"To the orchards! To the orchards!" the cry quickly went up –and the battle began. The horrible invasion blackened the sky. Locust covered the paradise tree, the posts of the stockade, the corrals. Their stench settled over every corner of the countryside and the orchards were transformed into dark stains of slime.

Every man, woman, and child ran out to fight the terrible plague. They beat on cans and shook sacks to repel the invador. Some even tried to shoo off the locust, but to no avail. The swarm of locust mowed down the vegetable patches and the flower beds, and all the women could do was shake their sacks uselessly and cry. Suddenly, one of the little boys shouted:

"Raquel, your plant!"

Raquel dropped her sack and dashed out of the orchard in the direction of the boy. Locust were swarming all over her magnificent rose mallow, her pride and joy.

"Quick, quick, hand me a sack!" she screamed in desperation.

But there was nobody around to hear her. In her mad rush, she had forgotten to run into the house and grab a piece of cloth –any piece of cloth– to wrap around the plant, so she tore off her smock and began to chase away the locust. The effort left her heaving, bathed in sweat. Her blouse was stuck to her strong back and her breasts heaved uncontrollably, drenched with perspiration. Only after she had succeeded in wrapping the plant, did she stop to wipe her face with her thick blond braid.

"Raquel, Raquel!" Moisés suddenly called out. "Come here and help us."

She could barely move, but she stood up and went back to the orchard. The fantastic combat lasted for hours. But in the end, despite the banging and shouting, the orchards were stripped bare and the locust invaded the wheat fields.

The sun was setting now, and the air seemed less suffocating. We headed back to our houses with heavy hearts. The slaughterer muttered silent curses under his breath as he began to recite the evening prayers. Raquel put her smock back on, and by the time Don Gabino returned with the cattle, the only sounds you could hear around the colony were the women's muffled sobbing and the barking dogs.

Song of Songs

For your love is sweeter than wine.

Jaime found Esther picking watermelons in the field by the well. She was crouched between the rows of heavy, bent cornstalks, with her skirt wrapped around her waist and her feet hidden by the thick undergrowth of melon leaves and flowers. The air was heavy with the smell of fresh, moist earth, and the yellow sunflowers shone brightly in the soft light. When she saw Jaime, Esther stood up and pushed the cut melons off to the side, slowly letting her skirt down. She could feel herself starting to blush, and could barely blurt out in a voice that seemed to come from someone else's mouth:

"Back from work so soon?"

Jaime did not answer. He sat tall on his horse, as if he had not heard a thing, staring at the panting and disheveled young woman lost among the plants that reached up to her neck. He took in her strong features, the way her full, firm breasts brushed against the stalks of corn, and the restless look she had in her eyes, black as freshly-plowed earth after a rain.

Esther knew the reason for this unexpected visit. Jaime had been pursuing her for some time. The songs he sang at the dances were for her; for her, too, were his displays of horsemanship at the rodeos. And she did not dislike this daring young man, who was strong as an oak and quick as a squirrel.

When she felt calmer, Esther looked up at Jaime's sunburned face and repeated her question without even noticing.

This time, he exclaimed,

"Look at this, Esther!"

He stretched out his hand to give her something that she could not quite make out at first.

"What is it?"

"It's for you."

The gift was some partridge eggs that he had found near the hill. Esther took them in her hands and Jaime got off his horse to help her.

"Careful! Don't hold them like that or they'll break."

They bent down together to wrap the eggs, and Esther's hair brushed against the young man's face. She could feel him trembling with excitement.

"Esther..."

A long silence passed between them, a long, anxious silence. Esther tried to hide her swirling emotions by talking about anything –anything at all– but she could not think of what to say.

"The corn in our field is nice and tall now, isn't it?"

"Yes, it is."

"Taller than Isaac's..."

"Esther," Jaime tried again. "I have to talk to you."

Esther lowered her head and picked at some leaves with her trembling hands.

"I've heard that they're planning to marry you off to a fellow from San Miguel," Jaime went on. "You know who told me? Miriam did. No, it wasn't Miriam, it was the mayor's sister-in-law."

"I'm not surprised!" Esther answered. "She goes around telling everyone that she wants me to marry her cousin, the cripple."

"They've also told me that the groom's father would

give your family a pair of oxen and a cow."

Esther shook her head, but Jaime persisted.

"How do you feel about it?" he asked her.

"I haven't made up my mind yet."

"Esther, I've come here to tell you that I want to marry you."

The young woman said nothing; only after Jaime repeated the same thing over and over, did she finally stammer:

"I don't know. Talk to my father."

A light breeze stirred through the tall corn and gently dropped some sunflower leaves on the young woman's dark hair. One slipped down to her bosom and its yellow tip showed through her blouse.

"I'm going home now," she said.

"I'll go with you, Esther."

They stood up, and a sudden impulse took hold of Jaime. He pulled her toward him and embraced her in his powerful arms. Then he brought his lips to hers and muffled the beginnings of a scream with a strong, firm kiss that rippled through the cornfield. When he let go of her, his arms went limp, and he just stood and stared at her, shaken by what he had done.

They said nothing more to each other. Jaime climbed on his horse and they slowly headed back to the colony, riding across the countryside under the warm sun. Just before they reached her house, Esther turned and said to him:

"Oh, how everyone will envy me!"

"And me! Listen, Esther, I'm going to break in my little white mare for you."

When they came to the house, Jaime called Esther's father outside, and announced his plan:

"You know, Rabí Eliezer, since my field lies right next to yours..."

Sacks of harvested wheat

LAMENTATIONS

Weep and lament, Oh ye daughters of Zion.
From a popular song

The women gathered at the home of Don Moisés, one of Rachil's most prominent citizens, to recite the ritual dirges. These were the days set aside to commemorate the destruction of Jerusalem. The colony took on a funereal look, and the pain of the tragic loss was etched on the old people's faces.

The elders sat silently on two wooden benches. By the light of the splendid Entre Ríos moon their sunken faces, white beards, and knotted hands seemed to form a mystical tableau harking back to the days of the Apostles. Who has not seen such gaunt and anguished gazes in medieval illuminations, or on the friezes adorning church walls?

Dear Moisés, your bent body, torn feet, and deep sad eyes recall those saintly fishermen who accompanied Jesus –Jesus, your enemy, Jesus, disciple of your master, Rabbenu Hillel. Like you, Jesus's followers ate of the bread of affliction; like you, they dipped it in bitter tears, as they remembered your suffering brethren, persecuted and spat upon in every place. Sweet Moisés, your pale face –as furrowed by sorrow as the good earth by your sons' plow– is the very face that glowed with joy upon hearing the Gospel long ago, in the days of the Temple of Temples, when young virgins elevated their bare arms before the sanctuary, and people gathered from the far ends of Judaea to celebrate the Passover, bringing offerings of snow-white lambs to the Lord.

Your lamentations now fill the sheltering sky and open fields of Entre Ríos, land of vibrant vidalitas, sighing love, and bellowing flocks, just as the awesome syllables [of the Sana Toikef] once resounded in the synagogue from the lips of the dying hero. And now, as then, no one will heed your call. Now as then, were Yehudah Halevi to recite his dirge at the gates of Jerusalem, wrapped in sackcloth and ashes, the mounted Sarracen would once again crush him beneath his horse.

* * *

"Mother, can't we start the service now?"

"No, it's still too early. We have to wait for the slaughterer's wife and her sister, and for the midwife."

"For the midwife? You don't say!" one of the old ladies exclaimed. "Why, she doesn't even know how to read the prayers. You have to say the words out loud for her, and then she repeats them."

"And to hear her wailing, you'd think she wrote them herself!"

"Many of the women are like that," Moisés's wife responded. "They can't make out a single letter in the Machzor, but they can feel what the words mean."

While they were talking, the men came into the room.

"Let's chant the evening prayers, then recite the dirges," Moisés suggested.

"Do we have ten men?"

"There are fourteen of us."

"Then let's begin."

Moisés faced east and opened the service with the traditional words:

"Baruch ata Adonai."

When the service was over, the women sat down on the ground opposite the men, and the lamentations began. Sounds of age-old plaints pierced the fragrant night air. Bitter tears, copious as raindrops, stained the pages of the texts, illuminated by the light of home-made candles. The sad, loud barking of dogs came in from the outside and mingled with the cries of the congregation as the slaughterer's voice rose and fell in a singsong:

"Like a widow bereft of a husband, so art thou, Oh Jerusalem... Like a woman who knoweth not the fate of her husband, who rendeth her clothing and walloweth in ashes and dust, so art thou, Oh Jerusalem, beautiful land of bounty, ravished by thine enemies."

"So art thou, Oh Jerusalem," the sobbing women responded, their voices resounding in the pitch-black night.

Outside in the patio, Rebecca was talking to Jacobo.

The girl's intense blue eyes, thick hair and graceful body sent shivers down the young man's spine.

"Why aren't you inside? " he asked.

"I'm still too young. When I get married I'll pray with the other women."

"Well, I'm glad you're not in there with the women."

"Really?"

"Yes. This way I can be with you."

"But we're together most of the time."

Jacobo was about to answer when the women burst out in loud crying again and the men took up their lamentations. They recalled the vanished glory of Jerusalem –Yerushalaim–, Throne of Wisdom, Crown of Justice, Kingdom of Prophets. Over and over they proclaimed Israel's eternal tribulations, their voices echoed by the dogs barking loudly under the moonlight.

"Rebecca, they say you have a boyfriend."
"That's not true! You just made that up."
"But you'd like to have one, wouldn't you?"

Rebecca didn't answer. Jacobo, bewitched by the aroma of the orchards and the beauty of the sky –the marvelous Entre Ríos sky– took Rebecca's hand, brought it up to his heart, and timidly planted a long kiss on her half-closed eyes.

Down the road, a neighbor was making his way back from the station, singing a mournful Jewish song:

A man wanders the whole world through,
He wanders from town to town...

Inside, the elders continued their lamentations:
"Jerusalem, shattered and forelorn, thy children's tears run like rivers flowing into the sea."

THE STORY OF MIRIAM

Rogelio Míguez and Miriam understood each other only through the language of song. Rogelio was the luckiest young man in that part of Entre Ríos. He was a renowned singer of vidalitas, much in demand at dances, where he would improvise love lyrics on his guitar with such skill that he moved the girls to tears. He stood out in his own handsome, rugged way, and had quite a reputation as a ladies man. Rogelio was not what you would call a "regular guy"; he always had the same sad look about him, and he rarely smiled.

The other hired hands, jealous of his conquests, would tease him for not knowing how to play taba. He had few friends, but the Jews respected him for his honesty and hard work. That is why no one was surprised that Don Jacobo Chalerman watched over Rogelio like a precious treasure. Don Jacobo, a hooknosed old man with sunken cheeks and a wisp of a beard who had been a student at the Jewish school in Vilna and a grain dealer in Bessarabia, was now a farmer in Entre Ríos. He loved to sing the praises of his incomparable farmhand, supporting his claims with obscure quotes and commentaries [from the Gemara]. He once even went so far as to convince his listeners that Rogelio would accept Mosaic Law if his limited intelligence [as a Christian] would not prevent him from seeing the light.

"Don't you remember the teaching of Rabbenu Yehudah?"[1] he would ask the colony's school teacher. "Accord-

[1] Rabbenu Yehudah Ha-Kadosh, the Commentator *(author's note)*.

ing to him, a perverse veil of darkness clouding men's minds is the only thing that keeps them from following Jehovah's Law."

Don Jacobo's daughter, Miriam [who hadn't studied Scripture in Lithuania], was much less interested in theological subtleties. She did not need rabbinic sayings buried in the Talmud to justify her feelings for Rogelio. She could not understand the gaucho's conversation –the family had just come from Russia, and Spanish still seemed as hard as a rock–, but she understood his songs. Whenever the young man sang a vidalita, she would respond with a Jewish melody. The strange syllables sounded wonderful coming from Miriam's lips; Rogelio's dark face would light up as he listened to the robust young woman with hair the color of sun and wheat. When Don Jacobo and Rogelio went out to the fields, Miriam brought them their breakfast. They would sit and talk by the freshly-cut furrow, bathed by the soft glow of the morning sun. Don Jacobo would go on and on about the plowing and the animals –about how many turns they had completed, about how strong the two biblical oxen were, tall as mountains and meek as babes. Each ox had a name intended to mock Mother Russia: Czar, Moscow, Czarevich.

"Alexander III has a sore on his neck," Don Jacobo complained.

"Don't worry about it, boss," Rogelio reassured him. Then, turning to Miriam, he added: "The coffee's real good today."

"Today work much?" she asked in halting Spanish.

"Nah, just foolin' around," Rogelio answered, and when Don Jacobo was not watching, he would flick little balls of grass at her.

Soon rumors began to circulate. People were surprised that Miriam, the daughter of a man as pious and learned

as Don Jacobo, would take such liberties. The talk quickly turned into malicious gossip. Little Isaac swore that he
had seen the two sitting together by the brook that cut
through the pasture. Raquel, the slaughterer's mother,
claimed that she had not only spotted them there, but also
eating watermelon behind the house.

Don Jacobo was aware of the malicious talk, but he did
not believe any of it, of course. In the synagogue, whenever his friends dropped him hints, he would respond
with Talmudic arguments that always led to the same
conclusion:

"Don't worry, Miriam would never marry a Christian.
Besides, Rogelio isn't a thief nor a murderer. You'll never
find missing rolls of wire or stolen cow bells hidden in his
room."

Still, Don Jacobo was a prudent man; he fired Rogelio
on the excuse that he did not have enough work for him.
That stopped the tongues from wagging. One Sabbath,
none other than the slaughterer declared that Don Jacobo
was an honorable man and Miriam, a fine young woman
–a fine young Jewish woman.

But the story had an unexpected ending.

It happened on Passover, when the entire colony was
congregated in the slaughterer's shack to pray in the
makeshift synagogue. All the young women were decked
out in bright, festive frocks and the young men stood outside arguing about their horses.

The early autumn air was filled with rich aromas, and
the flocks were resting in the pasture after a long day's
work.

Don Jacobo, wrapped in his holy tunic, was in the middle of elucidating some complicated passage in Scripture
with his usual eloquence, when one of the children shouted out:

"Look, everybody! Look over there!"

The colonists ran out of the synagogue, and what they saw horrified them: Rogelio galloping furiously on his powerful steed, with Miriam sitting behind him. The couple flew by as if driven by the wind, the gaucho erect and tall, Miriam, staring defiantly at the atonished crowd with her hair flying all around her. By the time the onlookers recovered from their shock, the runaway pair was lost in the distance, leaving behind them huge clouds of gold-colored dust.

THE HERDSMAN

Don Remigio Calamaco, Rachil's herdsman, was one of the colony's most colorful personalities. He was old, very old, and always on horseback, riding in the pasture or near the fields; his whistles could cut through the air like a hail of sharp arrows. He was tall and stocky, and had a wrinkled face full of scars, a shock of long hair, and a long beard that billowed in the wind whenever he galloped on his mount.

In his youth Don Remigio had fought under the caudillo Crispín Velázquez, and on rainy afternoons, when the water-clogged ravines swelled into rivers, he would tell his tales of glory to the Jewish boys who came to his tent. We liked to go there, to drink bitter mate prepared by his hospitable servant girl, and to hear his son pick out folk tunes on a battered guitar whose back the old man used to cut his tobacco. Those were Don Remigio's favorite times.

The flocks stayed in the pasture; the colonists did not go out to work. Don Remigio would sit by the stove, stoked by a piece of quebracho wood, and tell his heroic tales. Sitting on a sheepskin, he would stretch out his bad leg –the one injured in a rodeo years ago–, roll himself a cigarette, push it deep into his mouth, and begin to talk. And as he spun his endless yarns, his hoarse and raspy voice gained strength, rising in sudden bursts of emotion. Don Remigio never failed to mention Crispín Velázquez. If he detected any sign of doubt on his listeners' faces, he would swear that the sheriff, Don Benito Palas, could vouch for his every word, because he had been the sheriff's deputy back when robbers still roamed the thickets near San Gregorio. Naturally, Don Remigio could not read or write. His learning consisted of folk sayings, anecdotes about long-forgotten battles, strings of obscenities flung to great effect during the horse races held at the station, and pungent curses, useful for demolishing his opponent –always a cheat, of course– at a game of taba.

So distinguished a gaucho was no stranger to the art of singing and strumming. People in Villaguay could still remember Don Remigio's impressive displays of songsmanship at local dances, when the girls fell over each other to be the object of his serenades, and he would always capture the heart of the loveliest beauty.

His ballads were as awesome as his knife, whose silver handle had gleamed by the moonlight in countless duels.

Don Remigio was very old now, and living in a miserable, leaky hovel, but he could still evoke the years of his youth with a flourish. At such moments, the war stories would give way to memories of lost love. He would flex his bony fingers, and his sharp, thin face would take on a sweet and placid look.

"Juan, bring me that guitar", he would say. "I still know a little something."

Then, after careful tuning and copious rehearsing, he would begin his well-worn repertoire, songs that expressed the crude but pensive soul of the gaucho, his manly barbarism and tender love.

In endless, mournful refrains he would praise the beloved's eyes and hair under the inevitable trees and the inevitable moon. And at the end of each verse, Don Remigio would exclaim:

"That's how they used to sing in my time."

Like all old people, the aged cowboy longed for days

gone by, for the heroic deeds of his youth when he was one
of Don Crispín's men. His simple, generous soul was filled
with memories and nostalgia. Once the paladin of brave
hosts, he was living out the last years of his glory-filled life
reduced to the monotony of daily chores in the colony.
There were no more rodeos nor cattle drives. The large
tracts of wide open land were now divided into neat little
lots marked off by wire fences, and Don Remigio, accustomed to the collective spirit of the past, felt oppressed
under the new order. His fellow gauchos long dispersed,
his comrades from the great days now dead, he contem-
plated the foreigners who plowed the land and kept careful accounts of their calves and hens with hidden sadness.

His old age, as full of laments as his guitar, reflected
the melancholy of the defeated. In Rachil, he lived a simple life, breaking in horses for the Jews and helping them
to hobble pesky milk cows. He understood little of Jewish
observance, but he respected the humble, hardworking
immigrants. He knew that they did not light a fire on the
Sabbath, so he often went to the slaughterer's or the
mayor's shack on Friday nights to extinguish or revive
the fire in the ovens where the next day's lunch –meat,
and the traditional noodles browned in chicken fat– was
left to cook.

All of us liked him and were greatly pained when we
heard about his tragic end. The episode brought his life
as a proud warrior to a fitting close. It was so typical of
the gauchos of old, whose saga –the stuff of song– will
amaze future generations. Who can ever forget the horrible
incident? The men in the synagogue talked about it for
weeks on end, and the women still like to tell the shocking
story.

* * *

It happened on a Sunday, near the general store in La Capilla. The makeshift grocery was filled with Jews and Spaniards making their purchases. Outside, under a magnificent sun, the ranch hands were busy setting up races and placing bets. The brook looked like a gray thread wending its way toward the breakwater. Daisies and wild flowers dotted the countryside, and thistles grew everywhere, adding their own note of color to the spring landscape.

Don Remigio egged the young men on, slapping his heavy whip against his boot:

"Come on, Melitón. Are you man enough to race that bay of yours? Why, you're as chicken as a city slicker."

He pushed back his threadbare poncho to reveal the silver-studded belt holding his fabled dagger and boleadoras, and strutted from group to group with his tattered hat perched cockily on his head. One minute he was settling a contested call; the next, arguing over some point or other, all the while cursing profusely and mumbling under his breath.

Sergeant Rodríguez watched over the proceedings from his post by the door of the general store, yelling out every so often to quiet things down. He was in town with the sheriff to supervise the games of taba.

In the meanwhile Don Remigio had gotten into a heated argument with another gaucho, who claimed that his charger could outrun any horse.

"Juan," he shouted to his son, "come here and show this fellow just how fast this horse of mine can run."

The bet was made.

Juan got on Don Remigio's horse; Castro, who worked for the Benítez family, mounted his sorrel. The crowd of gauchos assembled by the finishing line near the corral to watch the race, and the two horses began their furious run. From the distance, the spectators could see the riders whipping the horses on and hear their shouts above the din of the galloping hoofs. Don Remigio's charger had a visible advantage, and everyone thought that it was the winner.

But just as sorrel was about to reach the corral, it buckled and threw Castro to the ground. A bitter argument ensued. Castro insisted that if it had not been for the fall, he would have won the bet. Juan objected, one strong word led to another, and before long they were going at each other with their knives. The crowd fell back, but Don Remigio remained calm. He slowly lit himself a cigarette, and said to his son in an even tone:

"Don't let me down, boy."

It was over quickly. The sound of the clashing daggers cut through the afternoon silence as the adversaries exchanged rapid blows. They were both skilled fighters, but mean and spirited in his attack, Castro soon bettered his rival. Don Remigio's face darkened every time he saw his son pull back from the vicious assault.

Castro, sensing that he had the upper hand, kept pushing him closer and closer to the crowd. The old man watched nervously, fingering his beard with his left hand and gripping his dagger firmly with his right. When he saw Juan falling back again, Don Remigio suddenly sprang forward, and with one swift motion plunged the knife into his son's head.

"Coward, don't back off!" he shouted.

Juan crumpled to the ground with a moan. Don Remigio turned around and slowly walked away in the direction of the store, leaving the dumbfounded onlookers to attend to the wounded boy.

Castro jumped on his sorrel and rode away as fast as he could. Whispers of admiration for the old man ran through the crowd of gauchos. He was the last survivor of an heroic breed of men; a breed of men steeled to bear anything –except lack of courage. Courage: the gaucho's supreme virtue, his grandeur and his song.

That was the end of our glorious herdsman, who spent the last years of his life in a jail cell, bent by age, burdened by memories and pain.

THE DEATH OF RABÍ ABRAHAM

The incident took place in Rachil on a cold, pale winter day. The sun slowly rising above the distant hills tinged the frost-covered fields in shades of pink. Whiteness enveloped the entire countryside, from the frosty house-tops to the icy paths, transforming that little corner of Entre Ríos –fierce and fraternal land of the gauchos– into a snowy winter scene reminiscent of a Russian landscape.

It was time to begin the day's work. Rabí Abraham went back and forth between the house and the corral, preparing to leave for the fields. The boys were in the kitchen, full of smoke from the wet firewood, downing their mates and stomping their feet to keep warm. Goyo, the peon, was stretching and yawning, still half asleep. And the old Jewish mother was out inspecting the hen house and muttering her usual complaint:

"Why don't they ever lay their eggs in the same spot..."

Between yawns, Goyo gave her his standard answer:

"They ain't been taught right, ma'am..."

Lapwings were crowing noisily out in the pond, and farther off, where the silver line of the stream merged into the transparent dawn, the loud whinnying of the mares broke the morning stillness. Little by little, the sun grew on the horizon, reddening the ash-white clouds that float-ed by like huge spots on the sky's metallic gray. The hous-es were now abuzz with activity. The Jews and their farmhands were yoking the oxen, still numb from the cold night air, and children were playfully calling out to their neighbors, whose loud voices they could overhear:

"No, don't yoke up the mottled one!" someone shouted from the next house.

Ruth came into the kitchen. Her hair was tousled and she was wrapped in woolen blanket that gave her unpolished, youthful beauty a wild and arrogant look. She poked the fire and joined the family around the morning mate, waving off Goyo's admiring glances.

Rabí Abraham began his morning prayers. Standing by the open doorway, he slowly wound one of the ritual straps of the Symbol [–"shel yod"–] around his left hand, and placed the other one on his forehead. He recited the benedictions with great devotion, wrapped in the tunic that gave him a solemn, oriental air. In the language Jehovah spoke to the holy prophets, he invoked God's blessings of joy and peace on his family and on the entire world.

When he completed the service, the sun was already high. The frost had dissolved into pearly drops, and the paradise trees and spurge bushes seemed to sway to the rhythm of the morning. A light breeze ran through the bare branches of the withered garden, and the air was filled with the melodious counterpoint of croaking bullfrogs and chirping birds [like a church bell tolling for mass].

Rabí Abraham hurried Goyo and the boys along. The boys ran to saddle the horses, and the gaucho went into the corral.

"Yoke up Manso and Gordo," Rabí Abraham told him.

Don Goyo reacted with a shrug and began prod the cattle. The cows nervously pawed at the frozen dung, but Goyo just leaned back against the fence and rolled himself a cigarette. He then roped the two oxen together, even though it was not necessary because they were so gentle.

That is how Goyo was. His only stab at work came at mealtime around the barbecue, or during breaks for mate. Rabí Abraham knew his man, so he came into the corral to speed things up.

"If we don't hurry, we won't have time to plow even four rows," he urged.

The peon did not answer. He slowly brought one ox up to the fence and started to put the yoke on its neck.

"No, Don Goyo, not that one," Rabí Abraham objected. "Yoke up Manso and Gordo. Chico's worked all week and he's not feeling too well."

"See here, Don Abraham, I don't like Manso. He steps out of the row too much."

With a patient smile and his meager Spanish, Don Abraham tried to convince Don Goyo.

But he would not budge.

Now frankly annoyed, Rabí Abraham brusquely pushed Goyo aside, and pulled Manso toward him by the horns. The gaucho's eyes flashed with wild anger. It was all over in a minute. By the time Rabí Abraham realized that Goyo had pulled out his knife and raised the yoke to defend himself, he was already lying on the ground with the gaucho's blade buried deep in his chest.

Don Goyo walked out of the corral as if nothing had happened, and disappeared behind the nearby houses. Only when the boys returned from the stable did they find their father sprawled dead near the oxen. Their cries of horror brought the frightened neighbors running. When they saw Rabí Abraham, the women broke out in loud, heartrending wails.

They lifted Rabí Abraham and laid his body on the ground, wrapped in his ritual tunic. His painfully twist-ed face, his open, sunken eyes, and his thick blond beard all heightened the tragedy of the scene, a scene reminiscent of old religious paintings. Rabí Abraham, with his long hair and beard, and his flowing white tunic, looked like Our Lord Jesus Christ, watched over by the elders and the holy women of Jerusalem.

Grave of Gerchunoff's father

THE OWL

Jacobo rode by the Reiners' house and greeted the family in Spanish. The old lady answered him in Jewish, and the little girl asked if on his way back from the threshing floor he had seen Moisés, who had left early that morning to hunt thrush.

"Moisés?" Jacobo inquired. "Was he on the white horse?"

"Yes, he took the white one."

"Did he head straight in the direction of Las Moscas?"

"No," Perla answered. "He was going by way of San Miguel."

"By way of San Miguel? Then I didn't see him."

"It's getting dark," the old lady muttered worriedly. "My son only had a few mates before he left –and he didn't take a gun along."

"Don't worry, ma'am," Jacobo reassured her. "You can ride around for hours in these parts without meeting up with any shady characters."

"May God hear you," Doña Eva responded. "They say that there are outlaws marauding near the Ornsteins' land."

Jacobo tried to reassure the two women again, and then rode away, spurring his pony to perform a fancy turn in order to impress Perla.

The sun was setting. A curtain of mist was slowly enveloping the waning afternoon, and the sky was shot through with pink stripes. The colors of the darkening landscape –the yellow orchard, the pale green pasture, the light gray stream– tinted the countryside in shades of sweet melancholy, much like the melancholy exuded in Hebraic poems that sing of shepherd girls leading their flocks home at day's end under the skies of Canaan.

The feeble sun cast a few dying shadows, and night engulfed the colony.

"It's late, my child, and Moisés still isn't here."

"Stop worrying, mother. This isn't the first time he's been late. Don't you remember how last year, on the eve of Passover, he took the wagon out to cut wood in the forest of San Gregorio, and he didn't come back until the the next day?"

"Yes, I remember. But he had a gun with him then. Besides, there's a colony not far from there."

A deathly silence followed this exchange. The sound of frogs and crickets disturbed the evening calm. Lapwings flapped about nervously in the puddles and a cacophony of noises rang out from the nearby woods.

An owl flew over the corral and set itself down on one of the posts, hooting ominously.

"What an ugly old bird", the little girl said.

The owl hooted again and stared at the two women. His eyes seemed to forbode evil.

"The gauchos say that it's a bad omen," Perla whispered.

"That's what they say, but I don't believe it. What do those gauchos know anyway?"

"Don't we Jews claim that the crow is a sign of death?"

"Well, that's not the same!"

The owl swooped down and flew along the ground up to the eave of the house. He rested there and hooted, then returned to the post without ever taking his eyes off the women.

The echo of horses' hoofs rang through the darkness.

Perla strained forward to get a glimpse of the animal, but her hopes were quickly dashed.

"It's not a white horse," she told her mother.

Sounds of singing came from the neighboring houses. Perla knew the tune. It was one of those sad, monotonous ballads sung in the popular vernacular to mourn the loss of Jerusalem and to exhort the daughters of Zion –the one and only Zion– to shed tears and awaken God's mercy. Perla mouthed the words softly:

Cry and weep, Oh ye daughters of Zion.

Then, in a firmer voice, she sang the ballad of the Spanish Jews that her teacher, Rabí David Ben Azán, a Moroccan Jew brought to the colony from Buenos Aires, had taught her in school:

We have lost Zion,
Toledo is gone,
Our sorrow knows no bounds.

Since her mother was still feeling uneasy, Perla tried to distract her by taking up their conversation.

"Do you believe in dreams? Doña Raquel told us a really frightening one a few days ago."

After Perla repeated the dream, the old lady remembered a horror story of her own [that had taken place in Kishinev].

A cousin of hers, who was as beautiful as a star, was engaged to be married to a man from their village. He was a wagon driver –very poor, very honest, and very God-fearing. But the young woman did not love him because he was a hunchback. On the night of their engagement the rabbi's wife –a pious and saintly woman– saw a crow. The bridegroom sold one of his horses and bought a prayerbook (*misal*) for his intended. Two days before the wedding was to take place the young woman broke the engagement. The following year she married a very rich man.

The memory of these events stirred Doña Eva deeply. As she continued her story, her face took on a mournful look and her voice lowered to a whisper. The girl was wed, but one by one her children died, and her household was plunged into terrible grief. And as for her first groom –the good man passed away. The family decided to consult the rabbi. He pored over the sacred texts and found a similar case in the domestic laws dictated by the Lord to the prophets. He advised the woman to return the precious gift to the deceased; only then would her peace and happiness be restored.

"Take it to him tomorrow night," he instructed the woman. "Make sure to carry it under your right arm."

The poor woman said nothing. The following night she set out with the prayerbook under her arm. She could barely see through the driving rain, and, sick with fear, she could hardly keep her footing on the frozen snow. By the time she reached the outskirts of the city she was so exhausted and so terrified that she had to stop and rest under a roof. She thought about her dead children, and about the groom whose memory she had managed to erase from her mind for such a long time. She slowly turned the pages of the prayerbook and studied the ornate calligraphy, as she liked to do in the synagogue during the holidays, when the choir chanted the ancient prayers from the days of Captivity.

Suddenly, she felt faint and her eyes dimmed. When she opened them again, she saw the wagon driver standing before her, with his silent, resigned face, his deformed body, and his hump.

"This prayerbook is yours," she said. "I'm returning it to you."

The ghost, whose eyes were full of earth, stretched out one of his bony hands and took the book from her.

Before she left, following the rabbi's instructions, the woman added:

"Holy soul, may you rest in peace. Pray for me on high and I will beseech God for your salvation."

Perla let out a deep sigh. The clear, calm night was drawing to a close. Off in the distance fireflies sparkled in the dark like miniature apparitions, sending shudders down the spines of the two women. The owl continued his vigil on the fence, glaring at the pair with his menacing eyes.

Obsessed by a hidden thought, Perla repeated:

"But if the gauchos say such things about the owl, it might be true..."

Doña Eva looked toward the corral, then down the dark road.

"Yes, my child, it might be..." she murmured in a trembling voice as her entire body shook.

A chill came over Perla and she drew closer to the old woman. Suddenly, they heard a horse's hoofs echoing in the distance. They strained forward, trying to hear, to penetrate the black darkness. They waited with baited breath for what seemed an eternity, hoping against hope. The sound of the hoofs drew nearer and nearer and all the dogs in the neigborhood began to howl. A moment later the women saw a white horse emerge from the shadows, galloping furiously. The mother and daughter jumped up, sick with horror; their anguished cries betrayed the magnitude of the tragedy. The sweating horse had come to a stop at the gate. He was riderless, and his saddle was covered with blood.

On horseback

CAMACHO'S WEDDING FEAST

For some two weeks now everyone had been waiting for Pascual Liske's wedding day; Pascual was the son of the rich Liske, who lived in Espíndola. As might be expected, the colonies' most respectable citizens were preparing for the feast, which –rumor had it– would be an extraordinary event. It was known around Rachil that the groom's family had purchased eight demijohns of wine, a cask of beer, and dozens of bottles of a rose-colored punch. Kelner's wife, who brought the news, had spotted the precious cargo near Balvanera when Liske's peon stopped there to fix a broken wagon pole.

"It's a rose-colored punch," she reported, and then added for the benefit of the slaughterer's wife, who was staring at her in wide-eyed disbelief: "That's right, rose-colored, in bottles sealed with wax."

Old Liske's huge fortune justified this display of wealth. He owned not only the land and oxen given to him by the administration, but also horses and cows. He had earned more than a thousand pesos in last year's flax harvest, so he could well afford to marry off his son in style. The bride was worth it. Raquel was one of the town's most beautiful young women –tall, with dizzying, sea-blue eyes, and hair so thick and blond that it seemed heavy with dew. She had a strong, slim body and full, firm breasts attractively outlined by her short serge skirt and blouse. The air of peevishness that she had about her only added to her charms. Many men had tried to woo Raquel, but she had spurned them all –from the administrator's clerk to the colony's assorted Don Juans. Pascual Liske was the most persistent, if at first not the most fortunate, despite his entreaties and his gifts. Raquel just did not care for him. All he could talk about was cattle and crops; she felt sad and bored at his side. Now, the young man from San Gregorio –that was another matter; he was so nice and he was such a good dancer. But her family forced her to accept Pascual and the wedding day was set.

The invited guests gathered by the breakwater near Espíndola, in a long line of wagons crowded with men and women. It was a splendid spring afternoon; the countryside was blooming, awash in sunlight. Young men rode up and down the line, flirting with the girls when their mothers were not watching, trying to outdo each other with fancy horse tricks and short races.

Above the din of the caravan, you could hear voices singing Jewish and Russian songs, and, harmonizing with the languages from far-off places, the strains of gaucho melodies, sweet and mournful as a wailing guitar. When the wagons moved, the wind carried sad verses about the massacre of Jews, and rustic couplets telling of a gaucho's love.

They arrived at last. The straw-covered houses, the procession of wagons full of guests, and the teams of heavy, yoked oxen all evoked a scene out of Scripture [in the days when Shechem went up to Jerusalem, and Hebrew elders, accompanied by their bondsmen and their flocks, made pilgrimage, singing hymns of praise to the Lord].

The wagons stopped off at different houses, and the guests went in to dress for the wedding. They came out a short time later, ready to witness the ceremony. What they saw amply confirmed the stories about the unheard of spending. A large canvas canopy, mounted on high poles, was standing in front of Liske's house. It was decorated with green branches and flowers, and hung with paper lanterns. Nearby, there were long tables set with white tablecloths and covered dishes that the flies buzzed around noisily. People swarmed everywhere. Old Liske stood out in his satin frock coat –a relic of the good years in Bessarabia– and a yellow silk scarf streaked with blue tied around his neck. He strutted from group to group with his hands in his pockets playing the gracious host, making sure everyone was duly impressed by the show of ostentation and wealth. And as if to minimize the importance of such excess, he would lower his voice from time to time and reveal exactly how much the whole thing had cost him, saying:

"He's my one and only son, after all."

The Hebrew word *ben-yuchid*[1] summed it up; that was why fat Pascual was so coddled and indulged. He was known by this name around the colony, where his loutishness had become proverbial.

Pascual's mother wore a huge coif, topped by green kerchief folded in a point that reached down to her shoulders. Moving her rotund body with surprising agility, she flitted from place to place, seeing to her guests and to the food –the real attraction at the party. A cauldron filled with chickens had been set up near the eave over a roaring fire. Roast geese, still dripping with fat, hung in the shade. A little way off, there were trays of the traditional stuffed fish stacked for cooling. But what the public most admired was not the pot of hens, nor the fish, nor the sides of beef that the peons were preparing. It was the jugs of wine, the fat cask of beer, and –above all– the bottles

---

[1] "Ben-yuchid," only son *(author's note)*.

sparkling rosily in the sunlight. Yes, there they were, exactly as had been rumored in Rachil –bottles of punch, rose-colored punch, sealed with red wax...

Two musicians cranked out popular Jewish melodies on the guitar and the accordeon, accompanied by singing and humming from the crowd.

In the next-door house, the bride waited for the ceremony to begin. Her friends were dressing her, and her crown of orange blossoms was already black from so much fixing and rearranging. Raquel was sad, totally unmoved by her friends' pratter about how lucky she was to marry a man like Pascual. Stone silent, she answered them with half-choked sighs. Her usual reticence had turned into a deep sorrow that showed in her furrowed brow and clouded eyes –her beautiful, clear blue eyes.

Someone reported that Gabriel was among the guests, along with the families from San Gregorio. When Raquel heard his name, she grew even sadder, and as she put on her veil, tears ran down her face and stained the snow-white bodice of her satin wedding gown.

Everyone knew the reason for these tears. Raquel and Gabriel had been meeting secretly for months; Jacobo –who always knew the latest goings on– swore that he had seen them kissing under a paradise tree on the eve of the Day of Atonement.

Pascual's mother came in, and as was the custom, loudly kissed and hugged the bride. She then announced in her screechy little voice that it was time to begin the ceremony.

Raquel remained silent. She stood up shakily, as her friends formed a cortege behind her, each one holding a section of the lace-shirred train with a comical solemnity. Her future father-in-law and the officiant arrived, and the wedding party went out.

The tables near Liske's house were teeming with people. Pascual, dressed in black, waited inside with his companions and the bride's father. The crowd outside started to clap and the ceremony began. The groom went and stood under the embroidered canopy held up by pairs of young men and women. He was joined by his betrothed and her godparents. Rabí Nisen pronounced the blessings, and gave the couple wine. Then the new wife, escorted by her godparents, began the seven turns around the groom. As she was finishing, an old lady called out that she had counted only six, so they circled around Pascual one more time. The priest {celebrant} read the marriage contract, drafted according to the sacred laws of Israel. He chanted the closing benedictions, and the ceremony ended with the symbolic breaking of the glass. One of the old man placed it on the ground near Pascual's foot, and he stomped on it with enough force to break a rock.

The crowd broke into loud cheers of congratulation. Raquel's friends smothered her with hugs, but she, silent as ever, barely reacted. Within a few short minutes, the main table was surrounded by guests drinking beer and toasting the newlyweds. Old Liske proposed some dancing before they sat down to eat. He initiated the festivities himself with the traditional Jewish "happy dance," done to the tune of the accordeon and the guitar. The bride and groom sat at the head of the table and watched the dancing without saying a word to each other. And directly in front of them stood Gabriel, staring intensely, looking very tall and very pale.

The crowd shouted for the bride and groom to get up and dance. Pascual grimaced uncomfortably; he did not know how.

Everyone waited with baited breath, when Gabriel suddenly stepped forward and offered his arm to the bride. The musicians began to play the obligatory polka. Gabriel tried to impress the audience, showing off his best form. He said something to Raquel, and she looked at him in horror as the color drained from her face. Some of the onlookers started to move away and to whisper among themselves.

"Gabriel shouldn't be doing this," Rabí Israel Kelner commented to the slaughterer from Rosh Pinah. "Everyone knows that he's in love with Raquel, and that she can't stand her new husband."

The slaughterer stroked his beard thoughtfully and smiled.

"I don't want to offend anybody", he said. "Liske's a friend of mine, and he's a good, pious man, but his Pascual is an animal. Did you see how confused he got when he had to repeat the *harey-at* during the ceremony? Believe me, Rabí Israel, I feel sorry for the girl. She's so honest and pretty."

Young Jacobo, the Rachil slaughterer's peon, took Rebecca aside and said to her in Spanish:

"Listen, honey, somethin's gonna happen here." He was the most criollo of the settlers, as evidenced by his coarse linen bombachas and boleadoras.

Rebecca seemed surprised.

"Listen to me," he continued. "This mornin', when I went to San Gregorio, Gabriel asked me if I was ridin' over to the weddin' on my bay. I told him I was, so he asked me if he could borrow him later on..."

Rebecca responded that he probably wanted to race the horse in order to win a bet.

"Races are the last thing on his mind," Jacobo said.

It grew dark. The lanterns were lit, and many of the guests went to see the artificial lights –rich Liske's whim. They had seen such a display only once before, when

Colonel Goldmith, the ICA's envoy, visited the colony.

The moment for the indescribable wedding banquet finally arrived. The guests took their places and the bride and groom were served the ritual "golden soup" in honor of their nuptials. Platters of fish and fowl began to circulate; wine flowed. The hostess's culinary skills were unanimously acclaimed by all those present.

"I've never eaten more delicious stuffed fish," said one guest.

"Where else could you get such wonderful roast duck?" the slaughterer inquired.

Rabí Moisés Ornstein joined the chorus of praise.

"No one cooks like Liske's wife," he declared. "You can tell that she's a fine person just by tasting her food."

Meat, and rice cakes wrapped in vine leaves, came out next, along with sufficient beer and wine to gladden every heart.

The bride got up. It was time "to go and change her dress," she alleged, and she quickly disappeared, followed by her friends and her mother-in-law.

But as Pascual's mother walked by him, Jacobo stopped her and said:

"Why don't you sit down a while longer, ma'am, and listen to all the compliments on your cooking. We'll be very upset if you leave us now. We don't want to celebrate without you."

"I can't stay, son. I have to go and help the bride."

"Rebecca will help her. You just sit down." He turned around and shouted: "Rebecca! Go and help the bride!"

The old lady saw she had no choice. Jacobo poured her a glass of wine and proposed a toast.

"When one has a son like yours," the slaughterer assented, "one has cause to rejoice, dear lady."

The clear night reverberated with the sound of glasses

clinking and the loud echoes of music and song. The sky above was full of stars, the air fragrant with hay and clover. Cows mooed in the pasture and a light breeze rocked the lanterns.

Jacobo got up and excused himself:

"I have to see about my bay. I think I forgot to unsaddle him."

"And I have to give water to my gray," Gabriel said, getting up as well.

Once they were away from the crowd, Jacobo took Gabriel by the arm:

"Listen, the bay's saddled and waiting by the palisade, and the gate's open. The herdsman's son is keeping an eye on it. Then, on the other side, right where you go out, there's a sulky, hitched and ready. The lame boy's watching that. Tell me, have you got a gun?"

"Yes, I do."

As he turned to leave, Gabriel asked Jacobo:

"And what about the girls who are inside with Raquel?"

"Don't worry, Rebecca's over there."

When the girls came back, Liske's wife inquired about the bride.

"She's with Rebecca. She'll be here in a moment," they told her. Then Rebecca returned alone, and she gave her another excuse. Jacobo proposed one more round of toasts, and the guests raised their glasses yet again. There was more music and more food. Platters streamed endlessly and wine flowed without stop. And in the midst of the frenzy sat poor Pascual, looking solemn and rotund, staring mutely at the bride's empty chair. Suddenly, the crowd heard the gallop of a horse, then the clatter of a sulky.

Jacobo whispered to Rebecca:

"When did they leave?"

"Just as I was coming back," she replied.

The bride's absence was worrying her mother-in-law, so without telling anyone she went into the house. She came right out.

"Rebecca, have you seen Raquel?"

"I left her inside, ma'am. Isn't she there?"

"No, she's not."

"That's odd."

The old lady told her husband, then Pascual. Panic spread among the guests. The music stopped, and people got up to find out what was happening.

"Where could the bride be?" they asked each other.

Rumors began to fly, and the slaughterer of Rachil asked his colleague from Karmel what ritual law stipulated in cases where the bride runs away.

"Do you think she has?"

"Anything is possible."

"In my opinion," he replied, "you grant them a divorce, and both are free to marry again. That's what's usually done."

The tension was growing. Liske got hold of the herdsman's son and asked him if he had seen anyone along the road.

"Over that way, goin' in the direction of San Gregorio, I seen Gabriel drivin' a sulky, and there was this girl with'im."

"He's kidnapped her!" old Liske's wife screamed hysterically.

Shock waves ran through the throng. Liske confronted Raquel's father and showered him with insults. Within minutes, they were at each other's throats, oblivious to the raucous around them. They overturned a table, and total chaos ensued. The slaughterer of Rachil tried to restore calm. He stood up on a chair and began to harangue the crowd. What had happened was a tragedy, a punishment from God, he said, but fighting and screaming would not solve anything.

"She's a despicable adulteress!" Liske roared.

"No, she's not," the slaughterer retorted. "She would be, if she had abandoned her husband 'at least one day after the wedding,' to quote the exact words of the law. I repeat: it's God's will, and they have to be divorced."

The slaughterer displayed his usual eloquence and erudition, citing precedents from the sages. There had been a similar case in the holy city of Jerusalem, and the great Rabbi Hillel had ruled in favor of the wife. [His decision is recorded and extoled in the Mishnah.]

The slaughterer concluded:

"Pascual, in the name of our laws, I ask you to grant a divorce to Raquel, and to declare, here and now, that you accept it too."

Pascual scratched his head, and in a voice breaking with emotion said that he accepted the slaughterer's decision.

The excitement died down, and one by one, the guests made their way to their lodgings, chuckling and whispering about the day's events.

* * *

As you can see, "idle reader," in the Jewish colony, where I learned to love the sky of Argentina and my soul was soothed by the sweet music of the land, there were Quiterias and Basilios as well as venerable rabbis and fierce gauchos. This proves that my tale, told with more veracity than art, is true –as true as the story of rich Camacho's wedding. May I drop dead right here and now if I invented so much as a jot of this wonderous narration. It would have pleased me to adorn it with couplets, like those adorning the divine book, but God denied me sufficient talent. So I give thee the bare and naked truth, and if it is couplets you want, pray add them for thine own delight. But do not forget to cite my name, just as Our Lord Don Miguel de Cervantes Saavedra did not forget Cide Hamete Benengeli's. If so exact a narration should please thee, send me no doubloons –they are scarcely enough for bread and water. Rather, send me some golden drachmas, or if not, I will thank thee a calabash of Jerusalem wine from the vineyards my ancestors planted as they sang Jehovah's praises. May He grant you –and me– His gifts of health and of good fortune.

Synagogue, Moisesville

THE VISIT

Don Estanislao Benítez's ranch bordered on Rachil. His land extended beyond the pasture, toward the station, opening onto fields crisscrossed by brooks and dotted with thistles. At the highest point, in the center of a clearing shaded by a sparse grove of trees, stood the venerable gaucho's ancestral mansion. Don Estanislao was one of the oldest in the region, a friend of Urquiza's and a comrade of Don Crispín[1].

He was one of the colony's most colorful figures. His heroic exploits were legendary; his lance, the most feared in the bloody battles of yesteryear. Now, in his glorious old age, Don Estanislao still displayed a fierce courage, outshining everyone at rodeos and cattle brandings. Like Remigio Calamaco, Rachil's distinguished herdsman, Don Estanislao was noble, brave, and illiterate. Solid as a proud old oak, he nurtured two great memories from his days as a soldier under Urquiza, which he liked to recount to his children whenever the family was gathered around the fire.

"When Don Bartolo went to see Urquiza, and we met up at the top of the big ridge, Don Justo said to him: 'This is one of the men the general told you about,' and Don Bartolo shook my hand."

He would then raise his hand slowly, as if to show the still-warm marks of that handshake, and his eyes would

---

[1] The celebrated caudillo of Villaguay, Don Crispín Velázquez (*author's note*).

mist over under his thick and bushy brows. He would then immediately launch into a story about Juan Moreira, whose exploits he had heard from his daughter, who went to school in Villaguay and often read the famous gaucho's adventures to her father.

"You know," Don Estanislao would say, "my good friend Dr. Míguez –may he rest in peace– who was a lawyer in Uruguay, once read me an article from a newspaper in Buenos Aires about how Juan Moreira died..."

These two facts gave Don Estanislao extraordinary stature among the gauchos. He was generous and kind-hearted; everyone loved and respected him. Don Estanislao was a good friend to the Jewish colonists, and he came to Rachil almost daily to watch the cattle being brought to slaughter. He would set himself down on his poncho by the corral, smoke his usual cigar, and engage in lively conversation. If any of the calves put up a fight, the old man would jump on his horse, throw his lasso, and in no time the animal was flat on the ground, bound and ready for the knife.

One day, Don Estanislao invited the slaughterer over to his house. Rabí Abraham accepted, and promised to bring the family. He yoked a pair of oxen to the wagon and headed for the La Lomada ranch with his wife and daughters, followed by Jacobo on his pony.

Night had fallen, bringing with it a warm evening breeze. The countryside seemed to breathe beneath the magnificent, starry sky. Gentle gurgles rose from the brook in the pasture, like a sweet music, and slow, grave bleats echoed in the majestic silence. Dogs howled mournfully at the round white moon mirrored in the milky waters.

Up on the road, the wagon wend its unhurried way toward the ranch. The team of black oxen, straining their

necks forward, kept a calm, steady pace in the shadow of
Jacobo's long sillouette. The little mutt Dum ran beside
them, merrily wagging his tail, rushing off here and there
to chase a partridge ruffled by the noise of the horse's
hoofs or the driver's whip. In the background, the breakwater cast its enormous shadow, rising over the road like
a giant camel's hump.

The travelers kept silent, fast in the throes of some
deep and hidden emotion. Was it the soft night air, the
blue sky, the joy of living surrounded by nature, their
hearts wide open to the call of the simple life? A bell
sounded off in the distance, the humble little bell of the
country church, and the slaughterer remembered that it
was a Christian holy day. The bell echoed once again, its
ringing barely audible from afar, but the vague music
stuck a deep chord in the soul of the Jewish theologian, so
imbued with the Talmud and with Jerusalem. A feeling of
beatitude swept over him; his nerves quieted and his
body slackened, overcome by a sense of boundless joy. He
turned to his wife, newly-rejuvenated by their sacred
country life, and pressed her to his bosom. He kissed her
gently on the cheek, and whispered in a voice choking
with emotion:

"Praised be the Lord."

But he could not express the thoughts surging through
his mind.

* * *

A pack of barking dogs met them at the gate. Without
thinking it strange coming from the mouth of a Jew,
Jacobo shouted out the customary greeting:

"Ave María!"

One of the young ranch hands came to quiet the dogs

with a few well-placed kicks and slaps, and when he saw that it was his friend Jacobo, he called to Don Estanislao:

"Boss, you've got company. It's Don Abraham with his people."

The travelers climbed down from the wagon. Don Estanislao greeted them heartily, and the women surrounded the slaughterer's family. Within minutes the servant girl was brewing mate, and they were all sitting and chatting under the eave –the gathering place for every weary wayfarer from near or far. Rabí Abraham, looking grave and composed, politely nodded his head every here and there, even though he could not understand most of the words of welcome and expressions of friendship. Jacobo did the talking. Playfully twisting the heavy whip in his hand, he first told how one of the reins had snapped during the journey, then went on to praise the taste of the mate that Deolinda, Don Estanislao's eldest daughter, was serving.

"I'll bet it's not this good even up in heaven!"

"What flattery, young man," Mrs. Benítez answered affectionately. "What flattery."

Don Estanislao talked with his usual exuberance, waving his hands and falling all over his words. By the soft moonlight, his bony silhouette, crowned by a sharp profile and silvery beard, appeared stately and venerable. With his lush beard, long shock of hair, hooked nose, and high forehead, the Jew also cut the figure of a gaucho. He was dressed in bombachas, like the natives of the soil; and like them, he wore a wide belt around his waist. Deolinda puttered back and forth, refilling the gourds of warm mate. Two magnificent dark braids ran down her back, and her chintz frock rustled as she walked. Her large, fiery eyes had inspired many a serenade from lovelorn local bards. And when she talked, her voice seemed to cut the air with its crystalline tones.

Rabí Abraham deemed it appropriate to praise his friend's daughter. After considerable effort, he succeeded in expressing his thought employing archaic and erudite turns of phrase:

"Don Estanislao, your nobility is reflected in your daughter's comeliness, for as one of our sages (of sainted memory) taught, only those worthy of spirit can engender beauty."

Don Estanislao did not fully grasp what the words meant, but he responded:

"That's just how it is, all right."

The women began to talk about their households. Doña Gertrudis sang the praises of her cow, La Gordinflona:

"She's as gentle as a baby. I milk her twice a day, once in the morning and once in the afternoon, and she always fills the pail. She never holds back."

The slaughterer's wife was astonished. Her cow was just the opposite –obstinate and hard to milk.

Jacobo knew how hard it was for his mistress to express herself, so he chimed in opportunely:

"If we don't hobble her and tie her head to the post, she kicks over the bucket, and you can't get a single drop out of her."

The conversation then turned to the hens' egg-laying habits, and Doña Gertrudis complained about the cat, who liked to chase after the chicks.

"That awful cat," Deolinda exclaimed. "Why, just yesterday it killed one of my cardinals!"

Little by little, under the influence of the night's sweet aromas, the conversation died down. The air was filled with the smell of trees in full bloom. Daisies covered the floor of the moonlit grove with a thick white rug.

"I've never seen a sky like this anywhere in the world," Rabí Abraham said.

He explained that had been to Palestine, Egypt, and Russia, but nowhere was the sky as deep a shade of blue as in Entre Ríos.

"Here, the sky is soft and sheltering," he added. "Even if you find yourself alone, out in open country, you feel no fear or trepidation because the sky radiates a benevolent light."

The old gaucho understood Rabí Abraham. His soul –the soul of an old troubadour– vibrated with emotion, like the notes of a hymn resounding through the glorious night, rising upward to the domed sky. Rosebushes sent forth their fragrance; hearts overflowed with the rustic joy of nature. The melodious music of the boyero, warbling in his cage, stirred the aged hero's heart, and he let out a deep sigh –a sigh that expressed his love for this land, whose cause he had defended with his brave lance and mighty musket in countless encounters, in forest wilds and city precincts.

He took down his guitar and began to strum with his thin hands. His voice quivered with emotion, as in the days of gallant preludes and Homeric combats. Slowly, the old ballad began to emerge from his trembling lips:

Entre Ríos, land of mine,
Where is there a sky like yours?
Your hills and your rivers...

Somewhere in the scented, soothing silence, a rooster ruffled his feathers noisily, and crowed his song.

WITCHES

"Do I believe in witches?" Rabí Abraham asked. "Well, now, that's a very serious matter." He immediately launched into a lengthy, erudite exposition on the topic, citing chapter and verse. "The Talmud says that there are two forces guiding each person's soul, the good angel and the evil spirit, called Satan in ancient Hebrew. So there's no denying these forces; the Talmud is very clear on this point. If angels exist, then devils must exist too, and if they do, they can incite impure beings to do their bidding."

The subject had come up because of a disturbing piece of news brought to the synagogue that Sabbath morning. It seems that at midnight Rabí Ismael Rudman had heard strange noises on his roof. At first, he paid no attention.

"It's the wind," he thought.

But a few minutes later, he heard the noise again. He opened the small window to get a better look. The short percale curtain was not moving, so it could not be the wind. Still, something strange was happening up on the thatched roof. Rabí Ismael decided to find out exactly what it was. He climbed up on the eave; from there he could see the entire rooftop. The whole colony lay spread out before him. There was a full moon lighting up the clear night sky. The animals were resting in the pasture and the brook gurgled on gently. The breakwater's compact black mass stood out against the silvery darkness. He could not see anything on the roof, but the noises came back just the same.

"There's nothing up here," he shouted down to his wife, Brane.

But Brane was frightened. She told him to come down at once.

"Who knows? It might be something demonic," she said trembling, and quickly began to recite the prayer to ward off ghosts. She was wearing her nightgown, her hair loose around her shoulders. Long strands of limp, faded blond hair fell down her back, and a few stray strands shaded her broad, wrinkled forehead. A soft gust of air ran through her gown, revealing two tired breasts that looked a sickly blue by the light of the moon. Brane shuddered, seized by a vague yet unmistakable feeling of horror.

"Ismael! Come down right now," she cried out again in a voice that did not seem her own.

Ismael, who was somewhat of a skeptic and little given to night fears, felt a sudden dread come over him when he heard his wife. He jumped down without saying another word.

That night they did not get any sleep, but spent the remaining hours mulling over the mysterious events with the window tightly shut and the door barred. The noises continued unabated. At Brane's insistence, Rabí Ismael took out the missal and read prayers invoking God's holy name to ward off the forces of evil. But the divine word could not drive away the evil spirits! The noises persisted, and the couple felt something dark and terrible brush over the left side of the house, sending tremors through the roof. Just then, a rooster crowed in the yard. The moon grew dim and a still calm settled over the countryside. They finally fell asleep at dawn, and woke up very late, well after sunrise.

"You must go to the synagogue," Brane told her husband.

"Yes, I will."

When he was dressed, Ismael threw the window open, and the room was flooded by the bright morning sun. But when he looked at Brane, Ismael froze with terror. He felt his strength give way, and he could barely reach a chair to sit down and catch his breath. One side of his wife's head had turned completely gray!

"Unbelievable," the slaughterer said.

"Just unbelievable," Kelner agreed.

"It's witches," someone else ventured.

"Yes, witches. That's what it is," another man said.

This led to a lengthy discussion.

Moisés Hintler considered the whole thing to be an old wives' tale. In Russia, he had always lived on the outskirts of his native city, and he had never heard such stories.

"I once spent a whole night in the middle of the forest, and even then I didn't see or hear a thing. As a matter of fact, I slept like a rock."

"That doesn't prove anything," Kelner retorted. "I'm not superstitious, but..."

And he proceeded to tell the following story. He had not witnessed the events himself, of course. But he had it on good faith, straight from the mouth of the rabbi of Tulchin. That was proof enough for him. Such a distinguished scholar would never deceive his fellow man. He was a rabbi, after all!

"A certain family from Haisin once set out on a long journey," he began. "In those days, people traveled by stagecoach. The roads were full of danger, so the frightened passengers kept their weapons close at hand and commended their souls to God. There were bandits everywhere. They would sweep down on the farms and maraude through the villages, plundering and kidnapping young women.

When they had gone but a short distance, the sky grew dark, and they found themselves on the edge of an impenetrable black forest. A shudder ran down their spines, and they asked the driver if they were in any imminent danger.

The Muscovite responded:

'There's always danger in these parts.'

The three sons gripped their swords, the old father loaded the guns, and the women began to pray. By then, the clouds had burst into a torrential rain and they were enveloped by the dense, sad night. Far off in the distance, the travelers saw a light. They told the coachman to head in that direction.

'It must be a tavern,' the driver said.

'So it seems,' the old man answered, trying to sound calm and assured.

Before long they were at the tavern door; but no one responded.

'There's light inside, and they're not answering,' the coachman said. 'I'm not going in.'

'It's the rain,' said one of the sons. 'They can't hear our knocking.'

A face finally appeared in the window, and shouted: 'How many are you?'

'There are eight of us,' one of them said.

'Seven,' the coachman objected. 'I'm not going in.'

The so-called tavern was a squalid affair. Tallow candles provided the only light. The walls were cracked and full of soot. Thick lengths of rope hung from the heavy wooden ceiling beams.

The pounding of the rain was more muffled now, but it was soon replaced by a more chilling noise that sounded like crying coming from the cellar. The men looked at each other and cocked their weapons.

'Could this be the Inn of the Tartars?' the youngest son asked his father.

'It could be...'

A long silence ensued. The 'inn' was a cave, well-known in those parts, where travelers who were abducted were held for ransom. When they saw the solid iron bars on the outside of the doors and windows, the travelers sadly realized that they had fallen into the trap.

The old father was a prudent man. He saw that they were about to die, that pleading or resisting would be of no avail.

'Let us say the necessary prayers,' he said, 'and invoke the aid of our ancestors.'

The rain had turned into a hurricane. Gale winds shook the heavy ceiling beams and claps of thunder rumbled through the walls as if they were inside the house. Hours passed.

Once, when they looked at the round windows, they saw the terrible face of the man who had opened the door staring back at them. Then they heard the sound of knives being sharped on a grindstone...

They began to pray in low voices, beating their breasts.

'God will help us,' the old man said.

'May He hear your voice,' his wife answered. 'I promise to burn fine candles before the ark (*santuario*) in the synagogue for an entire year.'

Suddenly, there was knocking on the front door.

'People are coming.'

'It must be the bandits.'

'Don't be a doomsayer,' the husband said to his wife. 'It's our saviors.'

The Tartars would not open the door. There were more knocks, and more terrifying claps of thunder.

Finally, the door gave, and a crowd of people rushed in.

'Come this way!' the innkeeper said harshly. 'This room is closed.'

The newcomers rushed by him, took the chain off the door, and came into the room. They were a large group of men and women dressed in elegant finery, like aristocrats.

The old man turned to them, and said:

'Thank God for having answered our prayers.'

'It's raining outside, but your worships aren't wet,' one of the daughters remarked.

'That's not surprising, my child,' the father responded.

One of the travelers had only one arm. He went over to the door and knocked loudly, calling for the owner to come and serve them.

'Bring us some food and drink, your best meat and finest wine.'

'The cellars are empty,' the innkeeper answered.

'I'll go down with you,' the guest said.

He came back a few minutes later, with the captives behind him. The crowd burst into cries of relief, into singing and laughter. Outside, the storm had abated and the moon appeared in the sky.

The family climbed back into the coach and continued on its way to the city of Haisin; their rescuers rode behind them in a brilliant cortege. But when dawn broke over the road, the mysterious travelers were gone and vanished, and the Inn of the Tartars was a tower of flames burning on the horizon."

"The rabbi of Tulchin, who was a wise and truthful man, explained to me what had happened," Kelner concluded. "The rescuers were the family's ancestors, summoned by the old man's prayers. He later came to ask the rabbi how he should give thanks for their timely salvation."

* * *

"And what about the Cross of Las Moscas?" Jacobo inquired.

Everyone knew the story. A certain man from Karmel once went to see Don Estanislao Benítez. On his way, he passed through Rachil, and asked the mayor's peon for directions to the old rancher's house.

"Well," the gaucho said, "go straight all the way down to the breakwater. Then, stay on your left, and keep going until you see a cross. Take a right, and a about half a league up the road you'll find Don Estanislao's place."

The farmer followed these directions; he saw the cross, and arrived at his destination.

But another man got the same directions and lost his way. He came back long after dark, and told the gaucho that he had not see any cross.

The next day the two of them rode out together. When they came to the site, the peon pointed to a spot about half a kilometer away.

"Can't you see the cross down there?"

"No, I can't."

"But it's right there, over by the bushes."

The settler stared at the spot again. Finally, he said:

"Yes, there it is, I can see it now."

The same scene was repeated with many of the colonists.

When Don Estanislao, who had lived longest in these parts, heard about it, he went out to the site. He confirmed that there was no cross, that there had never been a cross.

"That's impossible," the peon insisted. "I've been passing

by that spot for the last ten years."

He went to have another look.

"Someone's taken it away," he said when he returned.

The herdsman's wife was not surprised by the strange events.

"The cross on the road to Las Moscas? Why, it's the witches who put it up and take it down. I've seen them doing it with my own eyes."

From that day on, many people were afraid to ride by the spot; others swore that they themselves had seen the witches.

These witches were, of course, responsible for the mayor's disappearing yoke and Hintler's missing clothing. There were signs of the impure beings everywhere; what had happened to the Rudermans was proof.

Some laughed the whole thing off, saying:

"That's just what we needed. Now that we have witches who pilfer clothing and steal yokes we can call ourselves a repectable town..."

But the case of the Rudermans was no laughing matter, so as soon as the services were over the Jews made their way to the house. Standing at a safe distance, they inspected the roof of the miserable hovel. Rabí Ismael and the slaughterer were the first to go inside, and as they neared the bed, they started to scream in shock. Brane was lying dead on the floor, with her mouth twisted in a horrible rictus.

DIVORCE

"Rabí Jonás, why don't you present the case."

"I think it would be better if Rabí Abraham did. As the slaughterer, he is knowledgeable in matters of justice and the law."

The slaughterer demurred:

"It would be advisable to hear the opinion of the elders first."

The scene was taking place at the home of Israel Kelner, where the oldest of the colonists had gathered to act as judges in a divorce case. It was the first such case in the colony's history, so everyone's curiosity was piqued. Not one of the venerable beards was absent from the assembly; and standing by the window was the most imposing of them all –the Moroccan Jew, Don Moisés Urquijo de Abinoim. He was in the village on a visit to his son, who taught in the local school. Don Moisés, a thin, angular man, spoke classical Hebrew, along with some sort of remote Aljamiado {language} in which he expressed himself slowly and deliberately. Since he was well versed in sacred letters, Don Moisés was invited to take part in the deliberations.

Rabí Israel bowed to him, and said:

"Our guest should give us his opinion first."

Don Moisés Urquijo de Abinoim stroked his long beard and asked to hear the particulars of the case. Those present took their places around the rustic wooden table covered by a Sabbath tablecloth, and the deliberations began, as the young peon served mate and the lady of the house received dithyrambic praises for her pastries and tea.

"The representatives of the two spouses are here," Kelner began. "Rabí Malaquías is speaking for the husband and Rabí Joel for the wife. The couple has been married for three years, they live near San Antonio, and they are both honorable people."

Rabí Malaquías spoke first:

"Rabí Simón is not asking for a divorce."

Rabí Joel interrupted him:

"Let us record the testimony, so that the slaughterer can certify to its legality, and we and the witnesses can sign." He then added: "The wife insists on a divorce."

Don Moisés Urquijo de Abinoim, who was punctilious about observing the fine points of sacred law, requested permission to question the representatives. It was granted. He bowed down reverently, and asked:

"Pray tell us, honorable and respected Rabí Malaquías, are you bringing an accusation against the wife in the name of Rabí Simón?"

"I bring no such accusation before the judges," Rabí Malaquías responded.

"And you, Rabí Joel, are you accusing the husband in the name of the wife?"

"No, I do not."

Don Moisés rose and spoke the following words:

"Reverent gentlemen, we have just heard that sin is not the cause for these proceedings. Let us thank the Lord and praise the Most High for not leading us Jews, his beloved children, into perdition. This case, prudent sirs, requires careful deliberation. I do hope that Rabí Abraham will be able to guide us, and indicate to us what the law says. The couple in question is honorable. The cause of the dispute is not adultery, which is condemned by the sacred texts, but what Hillel, of blessed memory, refers to in his just decisions as 'everyday problems.' So I say that we should not allow the couple to separate."

Rabí Israel Kelner assented:

"I won't vote for a divorce."

"And I won't sign the testimony," the slaughterer added.

"We won't grant the separation," others exclaimed.

Don Moisés reassumed his solemn pose, and invited each of the representatives to speak his mind. Rabí Joel, who was well versed in theology, shifted in his chair, took the requisite sip of water, and began to expound his ideas:

"The wife is a virtuous woman. She respects her husband and attends to the needs of her household. But she doesn't love her husband. She was, as they say, forced into the marriage by her parents. The Iorudea[1] {the books} considered such cases, judging them serious, and prejudicial to married life. For a woman to live with a man whom she doesn't love is to be condemned to a life of unhappiness and suffering. Let us remember the teachings of the third book of the Talmud, the treatise on matrimony, whose sage advice was much admired by our most learned rabbis. In the book Nuschim,[2] the Talmud teaches: 'Should a wife stop loving her husband for any reason whatsoever, then she must separate herself from him and not accept his caresses, lest the child born of such a union suffer the consequences.' In the name of our Holy Law, I therefore urge you, honorable judges, to grant the divorce."

---

[1] Iorudea: jurisprudence, in Hebrew *(author's note)*.

[2] Nuschim: women, in Hebrew *(author's note)*.

"Rabí Joel," Don Moisés said, "we have listened to your learned words with great admiration. You have spoken eloquently, but now let us hear what Rabí Malaquías has to say."

"I have nothing further to add," Rabí Malaquías responded. "Rabí Simón loves his wife and considers her behavior exemplary. Still, he is ready to grant the divorce because the poor man knows that she cannot stand him. He doesn't want to cause her any more grief; besides, his life has been plagued by constant misery. How can one live under the same roof with a woman who doesn't love him? Since I understand how he feels, I join Rabí Joel in asking you to grant the divorce. Let justice be done."

The slaughterer requested that the judges be allowed to deliberate. And while the elders, constituted as a solemn Sanhedrin in the Entre Ríos countryside, engaged in grave talmudic debate, the peon came and went with fresh mate, preferred by most of them over tea. Ignorant of Argentine law, they sought to apply the laws of the Kingdom of Israel, bringing the wisdom and jurisprudence of Hillel, Gedaliah, and Gamaliel to life again in the patriarchal colonies of the Baron de Hirsch. The assembly was also graced by the presence of the noble and stately Don Moisés Urquijo de Abinoim, a descendent of the talmudists of the Spanish Golden Age, whose lofty language and judicious interventions revealed an intellect honed on long years of study. His grand manner and subtle reasoning brought back for his audience in the modest clay hut the spirit of disquisitions held in medieval Toledo and Córdoba, the deep and florid thought of those Jews who continued the tradition of the great sages of Jerusalem under the kings of Castile.

Fresh rows of dense Hebrew letters covered the parchment prepared by the slaughterer to record the testimony. Kelner invited Don Moisés to render his decision.

"The law," Don Moisés began, "obliges the judges to work toward the reconciliation of the spouses and the restoration of peace to the home, and I must insist on that, learned judges and distinguished representatives."

Rabí Joel and Rabí Malaquías reiterated their positions, citing precedents from the Talmud, the Iorudea {Jurisprudence}, the Bible, and the most authoritative commentaries and opinions. Finally, the slaughterer suggested that the divorce be granted, and the decree was signed.

"Such is the will of God," Don Moisés said. "We first refused to grant the divorce, as the law mandates. But after listening to the representatives' cogent arguments in favor of the separation, and after witnessing that the two spouses cannot live together because there is no love between them, we hereby grant the divorce, so that there be no Hebrew home where discord reigns, and so that peace may be restored to each of the sides. This we sign and affirm, granting to both parties the right of remarriage as honorable and worthy individuals."

Each of the judges then affixed his Hebrew signature to the parchment, using only his father's name, not his secular surname, in accordance with religious practice. As he signed, Don Moisés Urquijo de Abinoim took pride in the fact that Jews could always find justice in their ancient codes, which assure happiness through freedom. Imbued with all the power invested in him as chief judge, he closed the proceedings by proposing a festive toast:

"Let us raise our cups in tribute to the just verdict that you gentlemen have rendered, and let us also praise the Lord for having inspired us to walk in the ways of His Law."

"The Lord be praised," the elders replied, as they raised their wine glasses. Outside, the sun was growing pale, and stars began to appear in the sky.

"It's time for the evening service, and there are enough of us for a quorum," Rabí Malaquías said.

"Why doesn't our distinguished guest occupy the umed?"[3] the slaughterer suggested.

"It would be a great honor for me to do so."

"Let us pray, then."

Don Moisés Urquijo de Abinoim raised his hands eastward, and opened with words of praise to God, pronouncing them in the manner of the Spanish Jews:

"Baruch ata Adonai..."

---

[3] Umed: the lectern standing before the ark in the synagogue. Any table can serve as a substitute, wherever ten Jews –the minimum number needed– gather for prayer *(author's note)*.

Tale of a Stolen Horse

> Don Nuño de Guevara hath stolen my
> sword, but say ye that Don Moisés de San-
> dobal hath done the deed, for he is a Jew
> and liveth contrary to the laws of God and
> men; and let my Lord Confessor absolve me
> of sin, for it is virtuous to blame the dogs of
> Jewry, and not Christian gentlemen.
>
> *Don Guillermo Raimundo de Moncada*
> *Count of Marmila, Lord of Altota, letter to Don Felipe de Montreal*
> *(From old Castilian documents)*

Don Brígido Cruz's miserable little ranch was located several kilometers north of Karmel. His livestock barely filled his primitive corral, a narrow enclosure of gnarled wood built around two posts. There was a twisted pole in the center full of skin and hair left by the animals as they scratched themselves furiously against the rough surface.

It happened that someone stole one of Don Brígido Cruz's horses, a filthy, scrawny nag that could hardly move. The gaucho –whose shiftiness had earned him the name "El Ladeao"– never even bothered to saddle the poor animal, but rented it out to the brickyards to thresh straw. Still, someone had taken the horse.

One day, on his way to the butcher, "El Ladeao" came riding into the colony looking for his nag. He bumped into Jacobo, and accosted him:

"Hey, you little greenhorn, have you seen my trotter around here?"

Jacobo hadn't laid eyes on the horse, but he asked the gaucho to describe the animal and promised to see what he could do.

"We're neightbors, after all," he said.

That same afternoon, when he went to Balvanera, Jacobo made some inquiries, but no one could give him any information.

The following week Don Brígido showed up again. This time he claimed he had definitive proof that the horse had been stolen by Jews. He told the slaughterer so in no uncertain terms.

Rabí Abraham listened to the gaucho, whose breath reeked heavily of alcohol, without saying a word. He weighed his response carefully, like seasoned a talmudist, then answered in a polite and measured tone, gesturing with his hands whenever his meager Spanish failed him.

"Don Brígido, you are absolutely right in looking everywhere for your horse, and the sheriff should punish whoever stole it. But how can you be so sure that it was stolen by someone from Rachil?"

"El Ladeao" gave Rabí Abraham a knowing look. He wound his reins around the saddle-tree and slowly began to roll himself a cigarette. He shot him another look with his small, restless eyes, and finally said:

"See here, greenhorn, I've just finished telling you that they've filched it."

"I'm sure that you're absolutely right," Rabí Abraham answered. "The horse is so old that it could not have walked away by itself. So if it's gone, someone must have stolen it."

"That's exactly what I said," Cruz exclaimed.

Don Estanislao Benítez came by just in time to cut the conversation short. "El Ladeao" restrained himself in front of the respected rancher, and limited his story to the facts. Benítez calmed Don Brígido down and assured him that he knew that colonists well, that in his opinion none of them was capable of committing such a crime. Some rustler must have rounded up the horse and was probably hiding out in the thickets near San Gregorio. Benítez himself had once surprised a bandit holed up there with two lame mares missing from his ranch.

Don Brígido seemed convinced and rode off.

Don Estanislao watched him wobble away on his horse. He turned to his friend, Rabí Abraham, and said:

"There's a tough horse to break."

One morning, the slaughterer was summoned to Villaguay by the caudillo –"a good friend of the minister's"– to answer serious charges. He was accused by Don Brígido of stealing the horse.

Rabí Abraham did not show any signs of surprise. It was not so strange, after all, he thought to himself as he reflected on the situation. An Argentine gaucho may not be a Russian Christian {peasant}, but a Jew is a Jew –so nothing had changed. Is a horse missing? Then the Jew must be the thief. With the skepticism of a Jew accustomed to suffering for crimes he had not committed and to paying the price for laws he had not transgressed, Rabí Abraham now realized that the old tradition was alive here as well. He smiled at the functionary, took a pinch of snuff, and asked:

"Sir, are you familiar with our code of law?"

Mustering all the authority due to him by virtue of his dual role as chief bureaucrat and ward boss, the sergeant responded sharply:

"No, I am not!"

"Well, sir," Rabí Abraham went on unperturbed, "it's like this. The day before yesterday the foreman came to tell me that Facundo, my farmhand, had stolen a shovel. Facundo doesn't need a shovel, and besides, he's an honest fellow. So I threw the Italian out. You should have done the same thing with Don Brígido."

The sergeant, whose face was crisscrossed by battle scars and pox marks, did not answer. He continued to brew the customary mate, while his clerk prepared a record of the proceedings. When the accused heard the price Cruz had put on the horse, he thought of a way out.

"Don Brígido wants fifteen pesos for the animal," he said.

"That's right, Don Abraham."

"Look here, sir," the slaughterer replied, "I'm a busy man. You tell me that I have to come back on Tuesday, and we're right in the middle of the harvest. I'll give you the fifteen pesos. Why don't you send them to Don Brígido, and we'll consider the case closed."

And that's how it ended. When Don Estanislao heard the story, he laughed, and jokingly called Rabí Abraham a knave for finding such a quick solution to the problem. But from that day on the sergeant would always remark:

"They're thieves, those Jews. But I'll say one thing for them. They come out with it right away."

What Rabí Abraham had witnessed, perhaps without foreseeing its ultimate consequences, was the beginning of a new era in which age-old prejudices against the Jews were transplanted to Argentine soil. His solomonic stoicism hid a sense of fear and foreboding. The Jew was still the culprit, accused of stealing whatever was missing, blamed for every imaginable crime. And why? Because he had a long beard, was polite to his workers, and invited them to eat at the family table instead of out in the kitchen, with the dog and the hens.

But I would like to believe that it will not always be

this way, that on the second centennial of Argentine independence, my children's children will hear praises of Jewish pioneers sung under the cathedral's sacred arches, after the Catholic Te Deum.

Wait patiently for those days, my dear Jewish brethren; for patience, like suffering, is the ennobling inheritance of the sorry race of Job!

Baron Hirsch Library, Moisesville

THE POET

Favel Duglach was one of the least industrious colonists. The wheat on his plot grew straggly and the corn rose barely a few inches above the ground. Few hens pecked about his yard, where an old rake and a broken yoke lay uselessly near a narrow, crooked ditch, now a playground for the ducks that flapped around noisily in the puddles. The broken fence around the corral gave mute testimony to the owner's neglect. That's how Rabí Favel Duglach was, the neighbors said.

Everyone loved him despite these defects. Duglach was prudent, good-hearted and wise. Well-versed in Scripture, he spent his time talking to the old men in the synagogue [while mass was being said inside], going over the meaning of each prayer with a fine-tooth comb. He knew the legends surrounding the ancient supplications and loved to expound them to his friends in great detail. He would embellish his stories with abundant quotes and fanciful twists and turns, using simple language but charging his homespun style with visionary power.

He liked to address the women in poetic dithyrambs and often borrowed phrases from bucolic eclogues to sing the praises of the well-wrought furrow and the symetrically-bundled cornstalk.

Rabí Favel Duglach had the soul of a poet.

Jewish and gaucho traditions had fused together in the spirit of this thin, pale Jew, who was as moved by the epic paeans to gaucho valor as he was by the biblical stories that he told his faithful audience. At such moments, a strange light would shine in his eyes and his sad, frail body would come alive.

He cut an odd figure. A hooked nose dominated his face. He had long, wild hair and a long beard; a pair of bombachas and a battered gaucho hat completed his outfit.[1]

"I'm a Jewish gaucho," Rabí Favel liked to explain.

And he was. He glorified the nomadic gaucho in his direct, rough-hewn idiom. He knew all of the local legends and loved to recount them to the colonists on the Sabbath, exalting the heroism of the gauchos of Entre Ríos and the fighting spirit of the ancient Israelites in the days when Jephthah commanded his mighty armies, and King David spread his power and splendor over the peoples of the East. Once, someone asked him to explain the origin of one of the most solemn prayers, and Rabí Favel answered:

"Our people lay captive in Babylon. They pitched their tents on the banks of the Euphrates, which were guarded by enemy soldiers armed with cudgels and crossbows. Their modest temple, built near the city walls, was adorned with the sacred double triangle [custodian of the hopes of Israel]. And while naked courtesans danced before the princes and the priests, the captive Jews held fast to their faith in Jehovah's justice and elevated their supplications to Him.

One Sabbath morning, a strong, handsome young man came forward and knelt before the ark. He announced to the assembled Hebrews that the hour of their liberation had arrived.

---

[1] Second edition: His long wild hair and long beard gave him a bizarre mien; a pair of bombachas and a battered gaucho hat accentuated his absurd look even more.

'God took us out of Egypt with a mighty hand,' he declared. 'Now he will also deliver us from Babylon.' [It was the eve of Yom Kippur.] The young men of Israel surrounded him and made ready to fight. The din of clashing shields and hurling catapults filled the night as the accursed city lay huddled behind its giant walls. War cries rose up to the cloud-covered skies while the elders prayed in the temple and the King of Babylon cavorted among his women to the tune of voluptuous melodies. But the Babylonian hosts defeated the avengers of Israel.

The hero and nine of his companions fell into enemy hands and suffered martyrdom. The flesh of one was torn apart with metal combs, the others were thrown to the royal hounds. The hero's arms and legs were sundered and he was dragged to the synagogue at the very moment when the holiest prayer was about to begin.

The defeated hero asked for silence with a slight gesture of his eyes and started to speak. The dying man's voice resounded through the sacred precinct like a mighty trumpet, as he exhorted his brethren to fight for the reestablishment of their kingdom. He uttered his final words while he drew his last breath. And as he expired, the pious souls could see the shadow of a majestic eagle soaring high up above their heads."

When Favel Duglach concluded his tale, Rabí Abraham remarked:

"You speak with the eloquence of a preacher, Rabí Favel, and yet you never studied in a yeshivah."

"That's right," the storyteller responded. "I could never get along with the teachers. They forced me to memorize passages from Scripture and bored me to death with their theological interpretations. But my father taught me Jewish wisdom at home. Thanks to his teachings I learned to love life and nature with a burning passion. I admire the gauchos as much as I do the Hebrews of old because both are patriarchal and noble. They lead a sweet, simple life with their families and their flocks. Maybe that's why the slaughterer of Rosh Pinah accuses me of being a heretic."

Rabí Favel never missed a rodeo. He loved cowboy life, shouting his approval every time he saw a well-thrown lasso, a masterful horse jump, or a skillful roping. This sickly Jew often mingled with the gauchos, sharing in their work, roping and tying young steers as well as any ranch hand. He could break the wildest horse with the insistent goading of his stubborn spurs. And on rainy afternoons, Favel Duglach would visit Don Remigio Calamaco, whom he repected for his age and acts of valor.

There, seated around the stove that warmed the old gaucho's tent, he listened to Don Remigio tell his heroic tales and took turns plucking out tunes on the aged cowboy's battered guitar. On those dark afternoons, when the rain dotted the countryside with small lagoons and the whispering waters bubbled in the brook that ran through the pasture, Don Remigio's tent became a refuge for the hired hands, who whiled away the time singing folk ballads and spinning yarns. It was there that Rabí Favel told the story of the fight between the gaucho and the tiger. I can still remember the look on Don Remigio's face as he listened to Favel Duglach retell that famous episode. His eyes, half hidden by his bushy eyebrows, grew wild with emotion. Through the Jew's words, the protagonist's brutal yet admirable image took shape before our eyes like a sculpted figure slowly emerging from a rough stone, drawing coarse interjections of amazement.

His name was Pedro Núñez. At the time he worked as a hand on the Leguizamón ranch, which was bordered by a dense forest.

Tigers and wildcats roamed freely in those legendary wilds, where Pedro Núñez would lie in wait armed only with his knife and his poncho, hardly moving a muscle in his fierce, dark face. He would lean back, the poncho wrapped around his left hand, the fearful dagger clasped firmly in his right, and scan the thickets until one of the wild beasts emerged.

One day Núñez decided to entertain the ranch owner's sons with his audacious hunting style. The boys took their guns and horses, and they set out for the forest. A tiger had been stalking the area for some time, a hungry tiger, according to the gauchos who worked on the ranch. The hunting party made its way toward the woods, cutting a path along the brook. When they reached the forest the dog picked up the tiger's scent.

"Good dog, Blanco," Pedro said.

The tiger's eyes could be seen shining through the trees like two live coals. The boys cocked their rifles and were preparing to shoot when something so incredible happened that Rabí Favel's voice broke from emotion as he told it.

"No one was really in danger," he said. "There were four guns trained right on the animal. But when the tiger bounded out of the thickets, he made straight for Blanco. When Pedro Núñez saw that, he forgot about the four riflemen, and letting out a wild scream that echoed through the forest, he grabbed his dagger and saddle blanket, and went at the tiger. It was all over in a second. No one moved or said a word. The boys sat glued to their horses, stunned, paralyzed with fear. The tiger barely had time to raise its enormous head and to prepare to spring when Pedro, who was following its every move, pulled back his knife and leaped toward the beast. A terrible roar tore through the air; the tiger fell dead at the hunter's

feet. Pedro's dagger had pierced its heart. The gaucho slowly extracted the weapon from his prey's body, and turning to the speechless onlookers as if nothing unusual had happened, he said very calmly:
'It sure was a hungry one...'"
Duglach's heart was filled with joy as he told this moving adventure. The bravery of the gaucho –the legendary gaucho of old– gave strength and grandeur to his words. The colonists respected him because he knew how to inspire them with both Jewish and Argentine stories. He might have neglected his fields, but he knew how to praise their beauty and to recreate the fables of the pampa and the venerable traditions of the vanished kingdom.

[He is the poet of the Jewish settlements, and there he remains, happy and poor, still singing the praises of the Argentine countryside, his voice resounding like a rustic lyre whose heroic melodies extol the peaceful tranquility of the tillers of the soil.]

Revolution

In my {those} days the colony's most respected citizens eagerly sought the office of mayor. It bestowed a certain prestige and air of authority on those who held it, especially on public occasions, when the mayor had the privilege of shaking hands with the administrator or the special envoy of the "Jewish." The settlers would always be present at these simple welcome ceremonies, and the sight of one of their own conversing amiably with the distinguished guests filled them with a grudging sense of awe.

The high-sounding title of "mayor" belied the position's meager power and middling duties, which consisted mainly of bringing the settlers' minor needs and complaints before the administration –someone needed a new yoke, a cow to replace an unruly animal, a horse in place of the one left lame by a fall. In spite of this, the right to hold the post provoked ferocious battles, much like major electoral campaigns in advanced societies.

The mayor was democratically elected through a series of preliminary assemblies and raucous meetings at which the passions of even the mildest of Jews were inlamed by the jacobin oratory.

At the time, Rabí Isaac Stein was about to complete his term. Twenty-eight colonists formed a solid block opposed to his reelection; another group supported his bid. The situation seemed serious and ripe for explosion. The anxious talk around the synagogue was that something terrible was about to happen –and soon.

One Sabbath morning people were milling around the courtyard of the rustic temple and the conversation turned to the question at hand. Sharp words were exchanged about the humble officeholder.

Rabí Israel Kelner began to hurl insults at the poor mayor; Rabí Abraham, more serious and circumspect, nodded in agreement and stroked his rich long beard, and Jacobo –always a fount of information– shared a story that, he said, revealed Stein's true colors.

"Once, when I was at the blacksmith's..." he started.

Rabí Israel, looking very solemn in his long Jerusalem tunic, interrupted him with a fatherly pat on the head, and said:

"Children shouldn't meddle in politics. After all, Rabí Isaac is a respectable old man."

Jacobo shot back a sharp look. He tilted his hat back on his head, and pulled up his belt, shifting the polished knife and lead boleadoras. Then, purposely drawing out every word, he calmly answered:

"You're absolutely right, Rabí Israel. But if you say that children shouldn't meddle, how come you've asked me to vote for you?"

The answer caught everyone's attention; young and old turned to Kelner and stared at him impatiently. Rabí Abraham cleared his throat knowingly, as Kelner tried to force a smile. After a few minutes of pregnant silence, he ventured:

"You never change, do you? Always the same fresh little scoundrel... What were you saying, then, something about the time you were at the blacksmith's shop..."

"That's right. I was at the blacksmith's. I'd gone there to get a piece of fencing. Rabí Israel, who wasn't the mayor yet, was also there. After he left, the blacksmith noticed that a roll of wire was unwinding, and getting smaller and smaller by the minute. He quickly caught on to the reason behind this 'miracle,' so he attached the other end of the roll to a post and called all of us to come outside. Isaac Stein was riding away on his stallion at a slow trot, headed along the hill road. Suddenly, the wire snapped up into the air with a loud thud, like a piece of string that's been pulled taut. The horse came to a dead stop. Rabí Isaac flew off the animal's back and landed on the ground. He got up heaving and panting, unhooked the wire from the ring on his saddle girth, and shot us a look. Then, he got back on the horse and continued on his way.

That same night, he told me what had happened:

'I still don't understand it, Jacobo,' he said. 'Who could have attached the wire to my cinch like that?'"

Others had no less interesting tales to tell about the mayor. They reached the conclusion that his doings put the colony to shame.

"I asked him to have my yoke changed three months ago," one farmer said, "and nothing's been done."

"And what about La Rosilla? He still hasn't given me another cow, even though I've told him that she refuses to be broken and that I can't get any milk out of her even if I hold her down or tie her up."

Everybody had some irate accusation to make against Rabí Isaac. The chorus of complaints kept growing louder against the background of the sounds of praying filtering into the courtyard. All of a sudden Jacobo announced:

"Here comes the mayor now."

Rabí Isaac's corpulent figure came into view, as he made his portly way down the dusty road.

"Good Sabbath, dear Jews," Stein shouted amiably to the crowd, his face breaking into a broad, beneficent smile.

"Good Sabbath, good year," they replied.

Something about the less than enthusiastic tone of the response told the mayor that the tide was not running in his favor, so he decided to try to win over his enemies.

"Beautiful weather we're having," he began. "And isn't it wonderful that today's the Sabbath, and that we have time to rest and to enjoy the fresh air, and our young people can enjoy themselves as they please."

Israel Kelner, who prided himself on being open-minded, assented:

"That's true."

The mayor took this as a sign of encouragement, and that only loosened his tongue. He had a kind thought and a gentle word for everyone, and with his gift of gab he kept the torrent of compliments and encomiums flowing. The first beneficiary was Gintler, whose wheat field the mayor had passed the previous afternoon on his way back from the administration office.

"What magnificent wheat," he now exclaimed spreading his arms open with a theatrical gesture, as if the dense greeen waves of grain were lying right before his eyes. And what about Kelner's orchard? The mayor had something to say about that too.

"Tell me, Rabí Israel, in what other colony can the eye feast on such a sight? It warms my heart to see it."

"I also had something to do with it," Kelner replied dryly.

The mayor's charms even extended to Jacobo.

"And that pony of yours," he said, patting Jacobo on the shoulder. "Why, that pony would be the envy of any prince. He's priceless, you know. I myself would be willing to give you my best horse for him."

"You'd be making a bad deal," Jacobo answered. "He's a little wild, and you have to know how to handle him."

144

Stein, who had expected a more positive reponse, decided that it was time for him to go in and pray. He put on his tunic and stepped inside.

* * *

Elections were set for a month later. Kelner promised that, if elected, he would deal with the most pressing matters –the construction of a school building and a new synagogue.

He made this promise during a speech he gave at Gintler's house, in which he berated Stein for his ingratitude and indifference. He was elected.

Now, Kelner's old friends began to find fault with their man. Just like Stein, he took his time in distributing new tools. He was insensitive and full of pride. Once, the slaughterer came into the administration office to ask for his help in getting a new plow after the old one was destroyed by runaway oxen. It was sowing season, so there was no time to lose. The mayor had the audacity to answer:

"Leave me alone! Can't you see I'm busy now?"

The incident left a bad taste. The women were especially indignant at the insult to such a respected man.

"Who would have believed it?" they said. "He deserves to be punished."

A group of colonists decided to take action. The protest movement was headed by none other than the just-deposed mayor, Rabí Isaac Stein, who, in accordance with a venerable old custom, was now expected to lead the band of malcontents. These malcontents –just as venerably and predictably– included most of the people of Rachil. Soon, stormy meetings were again the order of the day. At one, people went so far as to suggest that the mayor be ousted, and discussed the best way to remove him from office.

Rachil seethed with controversy. The air was filled with loud arguments and heated debates. One day the mayor's misrule reached new heights when he dared to throw Stein out of his house. The town exploded. An urgent meeting was called for that same night, and as the young people headed for the fields, the old men huddled in the synagogue to ponder the recent events.

"Why don't we go to see the mayor," Rabí Abraham suggested.

After due discussion, his risky proposal was accepted. As soon as the morning service ended, they headed for Kelner's house at the far end of the tiny village.

The eight heroic elders made their slow way down the road walking in rows of two, beards flowing in the wind.

When they passed the first houses, the women came out with their brooms and rakes, and inquired what the reason was for this unusual procession. One of the elders explained:

"We're going to see the mayor!" he said, and pointed angrily toward Kelner's.

The women decided to join the line of marchers, and as the resolute column moved along its path, more and more women came out, swelling the enormous mass.

"We'll demand to see the books," one woman shouted. Her cry was taken up by the entire column:

"The books. Give us the books!"

The so-called "books" consisted of a notebook given to the mayor by the administration in which he wrote down the colonists' requests; it was the most visible symbol of his authority.

When he heard the commotion, Kelner appeared in the doorway. The size of the crowd alarmed him, and he asked in a wavering voice:

"What do you want?"

"We want the books!"

"The books!" the crowd echoed.

The mayor tried to reason with the rebels, but his efforts were useless. The men could be convinced, but not the women. His sweet talk only increased their indignation.

Finally, Kelner blurted out:

"Women should stay out of these things!"

"What did that monster say?" one woman screamed, as another threw her broom straight into the mayor's face.

That was the signal the crowd had been waiting for. The women broke into the house, destroying everything in their path until they found the precious notebook.

Stein's wife appeared in the narrow window, holding it up like a trophy. The procession then started back on its tumultuous way, brooms raised and rakes waving in celebration of the victory.

So ended the Revolution of Rachil, a revolution no different from all those recorded in history.

Settlers near their houses with an ICA representative

THE SAD WOMAN OF RACHIL

Anyone who passed through Rachil was sure to notice Cheved. She was so unlike the other girls. Strangers would slow down their heavy farm carts and rapid sulkys to admire this tall, firm-fleshed young woman, with the strong, hard look in her eyes. She had full, round breasts that pushed forcefully against her dress, and when she walked her proud and cadenced movements recalled the glorious maidens of Scripture.

Women like Cheved once rallied Jephthah's hosts to combat and serenely witnessed sacrifices and immolations in the holy city. And like those august women, whose images still adorn the fading pages of old missals, Cheved was blessed with a crown of thick, bronzed hair that made her dark pupils shine even darker. Solomon's canticles of peace and repose were surely composed in the shadow of such eyes.

Cheved was simple and given to melancholy. As she moved softly along the dew-strewn path with her jug on her shoulder, there were echoes of ancient poetry in her step. Young men would gather by the well in the afternoon shade to drink from her wide-brimmed jar, quenching their thirst while the oxen tugged nervously at the harrows and plows. She would then draw fresh water and make her way home, fixing her dreamy gaze on the long, gray road. She had a priestly air about her. She answered those who greeted her in grave, deliberate tones –the tones of a mystic–; the words that she spoke sounded like sacred syllables. When a neighbor on the way to work bid her good day, Cheved would reply:

"May God grant you many good days."

And the answer always had the ring of prayer. Thanks to Cheved the colonists' eyes were opened to the beauty of nature. She moved among the herd with her curved stick like a rustic image come alive, like a figure out of pastoral poetry. That was Cheved: desired by the handsomest of men, who nurtured visions of resting in her bosom and savoring her sweet, melodious voice.

Her father's house stood up on a hill, surrounded by a gate and a corral filled with cackling fowl and barking dogs. There was a ditch on one side to catch the rainwater, and on the other, a paradise tree, thin as a desert palm, where larks harmonized with the whistling wind during warm siesta hours.

And when the sun was halfway across the sky, dim and red, Cheved would take her sewing and sit by the shade of the eave. On some days, she stitched for hours, gently and rhythmically moving her bare arms across the cloth spread out on her knees; at other times night fell, and she had scarcely lifted her eyes from a distant, invisible point on the blue horizon. Her pupils seemed to dilate, and shine with a somber, mysterious blackness.

If anyone would come near her, she would shake herself brusquely and return to her sewing.

This spending of entire afternoons in trance-like meditation worried her almost hundred-year-old grandmother, who suspected witchcraft; it also worried Cheved's mother.

"I'm really afraid," she confided in the midwife, sighing fitfully. "She sits like that for hours. She doesn't talk, she doesn't hear, she doesn't see. Maybe she's suffering from some strange illness."

"If we only had a sage like the rabbi of Spikoff," the midwife said.

The grandmother put down the sock she was forever darning.

"Not the rabbi of Spikoff," she rasped in her wasted voice. "The rabbi of Vilna, Rabbi Eleazar, may he rest in peace –he was the one with the miracle hands. What a saint! May he plead for us on the Almighty's left. I've seen him free so many souls in torment."

She picked up her needles and muttered the appropriate prayers, the words whistling quietly through her toothless mouth.

The midwife tried to console them by citing similar cases.

"You're acting like two weak little women. The girl has a quiet nature, that's all, and she's not given to uproar. I'm not saying that there's nothing wrong with her. She might have water on the stomach or be suffering from lovesickness. Oh! How I wish I had daughters as beautiful as she is. Even summer roses and holiday breads don't come out as well –but I would not want my envy to harm her, God forbid..."

Tears of gratitude ran down the mother's wrinkled cheeks, and she said:

"May God bless her! She's kinder than a dove. How I long to kiss her children, to have them as a consolation for my old age! And my poor husband, he looks into her eyes and says:

'My precious one, my dearest treasure, you make me worry so.' And she throws her arms around him and soothes his woes with tender caresses."

That is how the old women talked until Cheved came by with her water jug or her herding stick.

They would then accompany her with murmurs whispered in the silent dusk:

"Oh, lark of my nest!"

"Joy of my life!"

"May God keep her!"

"I'd kiss the ground on which she walks."

The dog, busy chasing partridges in the pasture, would run at Cheved's call:

"Come, Emperor! We're going for water now."

On her way to the well, she would sing the song of the Shulamite {symbolic and popular song} in soft, somber tones:

I'll give you as a prize raisins and almonds,
Sleep, my Israel, sleep...

* * *

The talk around the colony was:

"Cheved isn't melancholy, she's just plain haughty."

Her rejected suiters said so the loudest, since Cheved had not shown any inclination toward any of them. No one had succeeded in getting the slightest smile out of her –not the gallant Don Juans, not even the rich Liske's son, whose persistent efforts ended in failure.

But Cheved was not haughty. She was good-hearted and humble, she helped her neighbors with their chores, she chatted with them and shared in their gossip. Of course, no one questioned her virtue, even though she often stopped to talk to the ranch hands. One morning, when she was coming back home after bringing breakfast to her father, who was raking the wheat field for planting, she gave a good loud slap to one of the peons working on the breakwater. He had dared to pinch her along with his usual compliment.

At dances and parties she was surrounded by a bevy of lovelorn admirers, but her answer was always no. A former student from Odessa had settled in the colony, and like all the other men he tried to woo her –with the same result. He would appear at her house on Saturday afternoons, and be warmly and courteously greeted by the family. He had attended the university –a distinction that sparked much envy among the local girls. But Cheved could listen to his discourses, ask him questions, cut into in the conversations he had with her father, and still show no interest in the new aspirant.

"What a great man, an astronomer," the women said.

"He studied at the university..."

"He still wears his student cap, and Cheved doesn't like him..."

Sitting by the doorstep with her chin resting on her hands and her hair half-covering her face, Cheved seemed very far away. She stared off into the distance, a lost look in her big, sad eyes.

On workdays she liked to go into the garden, stretch out on the grass, and lie still watching the sunset. This daily retreat in the waning light soothed her soul, parting the mists of memory. Little by little, she began to recall moments from her childhood. She saw herself young and happy, running and playing with other children along a gold-sanded beach in the picturesque city by the Black Sea. There, she was not Cheved, the rustic farm girl from Rachil. She was a fifteen year old in the bloom of womanhood, growing up in ease and luxury, lazily dreaming about the heroes in the novels that her father would read to her every night. The grandeur of those years now came back to her, magnified by time, evoked by the splendid vista of the dying sun.

She wistfully remembered her first love, the imaginary knight who wooed her in the late afternoon calm, beneath the trees of the garden, with the red-hued sea waves breaking restlessly in the distant fog. That was how the village girl spent endless hours: reliving lost dreams, recalling days gone by. The collapse of all that brilliance filled her with a melancholy unrelieved by the crudeness of country life. She found herself in the grip of a sweet stupor, a benumbing, yet welcome lethargy.

Neither Liske's son with his gift of oxen, nor the loquacious student could take the place of that schoolboy who had promised her the taste of an imagined paradise when she still wore short skirts and had braids. How different these men were, with their calloused hands and rude speech. Whenever Liske, or the student, or the slaughterer's brother tried to murmur sweet nothings in her ears, she secretly compared him with the dashing young man of her childhood years. What was he doing now? she wondered.

In the thickening shadows, the thistle bushes looked like growths in a fantastic jungle. Cows' mooing reverberated through the air. From their ponds, frogs croaked their sad ballads, and far, far off in the distance the herdsman's cries announced that the hour of rest had arrived.

Cheved remained lost in thought. What was her love doing now? She pictured him handsome and triumphant, pursued by the city's most beautiful women. The image that she conjured up was one of unmatched splendor. How magnificent those women were in their low-cut ball gowns. How she envied their clothes, their perfume, their silky white skin. Yes, they were worthy companions to her first true love, her knight in shining armor. How they surrounded and toasted him in the elegant salons. The sounds of their laughter and their party chatter seemed to reach her in the midst of her enrapture. Her lover looked so arrogant, so desired by the ladies.

Once, when she was thinking about him, she had trouble remembering his name. She tried a few names under her breath, but each time shook her head. It finally came to her, and when she said it out loud, the joyous echo of its syllables roused her from her reverie.

* * *

She was walking back along the winding path, when she heard Lázaro behind her, playing his clay flute. Never had the rustic instrument's mournful notes sounded so sad, so plaintive. Cheved turned around and said:

"Lázaro, you play just like a musician."

The hulking young man stopped and steadied his lame leg, then smiled at her without moving the flute away from his lips. He continued to play as they made their way back together.

Streaks of red crisscrossed the horizon. A deep silence had settled over the countryside, broken only by the chirping crickets and barking dogs. The sleepy, languid afternoon was gently slipping into night. High above their heads, a sliver of a moon appeared and pale stars began to show between the serene clouds.

"Why did you stop playing?" Cheved asked Lázaro.

"I didn't think you liked it," he answered.

"Oh, but I do, and especially this afternoon."

The young farmer began to play a tune, one of his repertoire of Russian songs, Jewish melodies, vidalitas, and estilos. The lame piper's music, echoing through the valley, soothed Cheved's soul, slowly drawing her away from her visions of the past. They walked for hours without saying a word. It was almost night when she told him:

"I have to go now. They're expecting me at home. Come by tomorrow."

Lázaro wanted to say something. He blushed and riveted his eyes on the young woman, but his throat knotted and nothing came out. He tried to calm himself so that Cheved would not notice his embarrassment, and finally managed to blurt out before they separated:

"Don't forget to give my regards to Rabí Jonás."

After dinner, Rabí Jonás read aloud from one of Schummer's novels. Cheved was always moved by the subject –the persecution of the Jews in Spain.

She thought about the protagonist, the grandee Don Pedro de Parera, whom the author dressed in velvet and placed among the princes and princesses of the court of the Philips. Her brow clouded as she reflected on how different real men were from men in books. What would Don Pedro be like if he were real? What kind of man was the author, Schummer? And what about the love of her youth? What was he like now? But as she asked herself this question, she found his image, once so dear to her, fading from her memory.

She dozed off, and her dreams were filled with Lázaro's tremulous melodies sounding again from his simple clay flute, calming her anxious spirit as they had done in the slow and sleepy country afternoon.

The next day, secreted in her garden hideaway, she felt more at peace. Would Lázaro come? she wondered. She had never paid much attention to the sweet young man. How well he played! She now saw his image, with his leg, reflected everywhere –in the blue sky, the nearby bushes, the black earth stretched out in neat furrows as far as the eye could see. She remembered one time when Lázaro could not catch a calf that had broken loose. The sight of the lame musician dragging his bad leg had so upset her that she had rushed after the animal and brought it back. She could not forget how overwhelmed with emotion

Lázaro had been, how he could not find the words to thank her. Her heart was filled with deep compassion.

Cheved compared Lázaro to her other suitors, to the brutish Liske, and the student –so talkative and so insistent. Neither of them was worth as much as the simple, unaffected Lázaro. He had never said a word to her, but he was there, wherever she went, contemplating her with his eloquent muteness.

Would he come today? She felt herself growing impatient, eaten by doubt. Soon she could think of nothing else.

When the sounds of the hersdman bringing in the flocks died down, and she heard the familiar sound of a flute, she jumped up, and without realizing what she was doing, began to wave and cry jubilantly:

"Lázaro! Lázaro!"

Before the service

THE OLD COLONIST

Here lies interred a virtuous elder, who
'neath this stone awaits, in just reward,
the coming resurrection and Messiah. The
good Lord, blessed be His Name, called
him full of years to enjoy everlasting
Heaven.

Inscription in Aljamiado

Let us call him by his biblical name, Rabí Gedalí. Let us
forget his surname, surely composed in some eighteenth-
century German city by high-born gentlemen to mock the
Jewish rag dealers crowding the sordid ghettos of Frank-
furt or Munich. Gedalí, or better yet, in talmudic fashion,
Rabí Gedalí ben Shelomo. He deserved to be addressed in
this manner because his proud bearing –far from suggest-
ing a humble farmer– recalled the noble eras when
Hebrew poets and sages formed learned guilds in the
towns of medieval Spain. Only those Jews mentioned by
Rabí Menashe ben Israel in his writings bore any resem-
blance to Gedalí. He was tall and stately, and had a patri-
cian air, like a figure out of an old engraving. His pale face
bespoke long hours spent in meditation; the smile that
danced around his lips hid the scars of suffering.

He was my teacher. I learned the meaning of the
prayers and the use of the Symbols under the angled roof
of his rustic cottage. All of us respected him because he
was worthy of respect.

I met Rabí Gedalí when he was already old. He went
to synagogue every morning and every afternoon, walk-

ing lost in thought, leaning on a curved walking stick like a patriarch on his staff. He was wise and gentle in the way of those who have lived long and seen much. He no longer worked, but spent his days inculcating God's wisdom in the young, thanking the Lord for His bounties, and comforting the dying in their final hours. That is why I've honored his memory with the words of an epitaph composed in Aljamiado by an anonymous poet to eulogize the great Rashi; they are inscribed in an old prayer book (*misal*) from Constantinople. I'd also like to repeat what my mother always said at the Passover table whenever she told us an story about the sage's exemplary life:

"May my words not disturb his eternal rest!"

* * *

Rabí Gedalí had a grave and majestic bearing. Old age had spiritualized the once-solid outlines of his body, and his slow step gave him a priestly presence. He seemed to be offering a blessing every time he raised his thin, trembling hand, and when he prayed –his head turned to God, his bearded face radiant with the light of the divine– he brought to mind those ancient masters whose lives and works contain eternal truths.

One day we saw him coming toward our house. He came in and greeted us in the Hebraic mode, as he always did:

"God grant that I bring good fortune to your home."

He caught his breath, inhaled a pinch of snuff picked from a worn box decorated with a faded Old Testament scene, and after the requisite nicities about our shimmering wheat and wonderful cow, he announced to my mother that he had come on a very important mission.

"Madam," he began, "your son is an orphan and he has to be taught our doctrines, because orphans are confirmed at the age of twelve. It would give me great pleasure to teach him our holy alphabet, so that he can pray for his dear ones and give thanks to the Lord."

From that day on, as soon as I turned the cattle to pasture, I would go to Rabí Gedalí's house. The tongue of the prophets and rabbis flowed from his lips, pristine and melodious, and after we had rehearsed the prayers, he would explain the meaning of the psalms and the talmudic literature. He would cite fine points of morals and theology, following Ibn Gabirol ben Yehudah and other Spanish and Arab Hebraists, then quote tender fables from the poets. He navigated easily in this deep and perplexing sea of writing, and his keen intellect, honed on the study of sacred texts, unlocked the secrets of the Gemara and the Kabbalah. Rabí Gedalí once taught me:

"He who does not possess a wise mind and a kind heart is like someone who has only one eye and can see only in one direction. My son, let me tell you about a case that sparked heated debate in the days when our brethren lived peacefully under the protection of the kings of Castile."

"Rabbi Akiva asked his disciples: What does a man need to attain true happiness? One disciple responded: A close and devoted friend. Another said: Good health. A third: Intelligence. A fourth: Wisdom."

"When Rabbi Akiva remained silent, the disciple who had not yet spoken ventured an answer: All of these qualities. For just as a ray of light is the sum of all the colors of the rainbow, so do all these blessings together give a man the means to confront any woe, even if he be in the remotest corner of the earth."

"Do you understand, my son?" Rabí Gedalí concluded. "Now, let us begin the evening prayer, lest the dinner hour arrive before we have properly praised God."

* * *

Whenever his children and grandchildren cut the first furrow in their fields, Rabí Gedalí would guide the plow. For him, it was a solemn, inaugural act, and he invested it with the same religious aura that planting had in the Talmud. He would put on his thick fur greatcoat, and after the field had been marked and flagged, he would take the plow and guide the oxen in the sacred task of breaking the hard earth. When this brief ceremony was over, he would sit on a rock and watch the young men at work, shouting out words of encouragement:

"Remember, Abraham, my son, remember, Jacob, my treasure, it may be difficult to bring forth bread from the earth, but that is the way of honorable men. If my hands had only held the prayerbook and the plow, I would now be destined to watch over you in Paradise!"

He would then go back to his modest straw hut, where his wife was warming her old body by the fire, and say to her:

"I've left our children in the field. They do us honor with the sweat of their brow. May God grant us a good year, and may those less fortunate have a good year too! Have you prayed and eaten yet?"

On the day I was confirmed, the neighbors came to our house to extend their good wishes and share in the traditional sweet cakes and wine. That is when I heard Rabí Gedalí tell the story of his life.

This kindly old man, now so immersed in religion and prayer, had once founded a city in Russia. He had made a fortune as a young man when the peasants were still serfs of the landowners. Those were the days when the czar's soldiers roamed the countryside in the empire's Polish provinces, looting and killing. They would kidnap the local princes, string them up in the town squares, and then, rumor had it, sell their clothing and jewels to Austrian traffickers. That was when Rabí Gedalí acquired large tracts of land. Unlike the other landowners, he let the peasants enjoy the benefits of their labor. This led imperial officials to accuse him before the court as a disturber of the peace and an enemy of the state. But Rabí Gedalí was not afraid. He went to St. Petersburg to put his case before the czar himself, bringing an antique Pentateuch and a string of pearls as gifts.

"Here is a good Jew," Czar Nicholas said. "He deserves our respect." And he granted Rabí Gedalí the same rights given to the nobility.

But when serfdom was abolished his land was taken away. He suffered even greater setbacks during the wars undertaken by Czar Alexander II. He was still rich, however, and continued to live in the city he had founded, until he heard news of America. He made a pilgrimage to Jerusalem but came back disillusioned, saying that he preferred to be anywhere else than to see the sorry state of the holy city, where Jews were surrounded by convents and crosses {and mosques}. So he decided to leave his possessions behind and come to Entre Ríos. He was among the first immigrants to the colonies, where he fulfilled his lifelong dream of tilling the soil and eating the fruits of his garden and field.

Early one morning a boy came say that Rabí Gedalí was asking for us. We rushed over, sensing that his end was near. The house was full of people, but Rabí Gedalí sat in the middle of the crowd looking calm and imposing in his kitol[1] {white tunic}. His life was ebbing like a flickering candle. He took leave of each one of us, lifted his eyes toward heaven, and uttered these parting words:

"May your bodies, like mine, find eternal rest in the very earth on which you toil. Then shall you be truly blessed."

He grew silent and his eyes closed as the gathered crowd burst into loud lamentation. That is how my beloved teacher lived and died.

[[1] Kitol: a white linen gown worn during the ritual Passover meal, and by those about to die. It is wrapped around the body before burial (author's note).]

THE ANTHEM

In the early days of the colony the Jews knew very little about Entre Ríos and had very sketchy notions about local customs. They both feared and admired the gaucho, surrounding his way of life with a vague aura of lawlessness and heroism. The novice farmers saw the gaucho as a dangerous and angry outlaw. This view was reinforced by the tales of blood and bravery told on moonlit nights by the few bards who still sang of the pampa horseman's glory –tales the newcomers barely understood. In the eyes of the recent immigrants from Poland or Bessarabia, the gaucho seemed like a noble bandit, a ferocious but romantic hero straight out of the pages of a novel by Schummer, whose adventures the young working women devoured after a day's work in the factories of Odessa or the colony's fields and orchards.

In those first years young and old alike would congregate in Rachil's makeshift synagogue to talk about Argentina. Their enthusiasm for their new life –a life only dreamed about in the bitter old days in Russia– still had not waned. Every heart overflowed with love, every eye glistened with hope. All around Rachil, plows joyfully turned the earth and sounds of song filled the air. On Sabbath mornings the settlers would gather outside the synagogue and tell stories of their slavery and exodus, as if the emigration from the Russian Empire were the biblical flight from Egypt narrated on the eve of the Passover.

They held different opinions about the new land. José Haler, who had done military service in Russia, maintained that Argentina had no army. But Rabí Isaac Herman, a frail old man who taught the colony's children how to pray, vehemently rebutted this assertion:

"What do you know? You're just a little soldier boy," he taunted poor José. "How can you say that Argentina has no army? Aren't there soldiers in Russia, even though it's a monarchy?"

"Well, that's exactly the point, Rabí Isaac," José answered. "Here the czar is a president, and he doesn't need soldiers to protect him."

"And what about the soldiers we see in Domínguez?"

The old man's question unsettled José. He could not explain what the sergeant, whose curved saber spread terror among the children, was doing in the Domínguez train station.

One afternoon, a farmer returning from Villaguay brought word of an upcoming holiday. He reported that the main street was decorated with arches and flags. The news spread rapidly, until another colonist finally suggested that they find out the reason for the celebration.

The settlers did not speak a word of Spanish. The young men had quickly picked up the gauchos' dress and manners, but they could barely communicate with the locals. Still, they decided to consult the colony's herdsman, Don Gabino, a veteran of the Paraguay Campaign who had fought with Crispín Velázquez. Don Gabino thought that the preparations might be for a rodeo or an election campaign. Although this seemed to make sense, Don Benito Palas, the colony's police chief, cleared up the mystery when he explained to the slaughterer that May 25th was Argentine Independence Day.

The patriotic date became the colonists' main topic of

conversation at their nightly gatherings and during breaks from work. In the end, on the initiative of Israel Kelner, they voted to hold a celebration.

Kelner, who had been to Jerusalem as the delegate from Zhitomir to organize the emigration of 1889, was a repected Hebraist and a skilled orator, publicly acclaimed by the slaughterers of Karmel and Rachil. He went to Don Estanislao Benítez's ranch in Las Moscas to receive detailed information about the matter.

The settlers decided to proceed, and appointed the mayor and the slaughterer to organize the festivities. Rabí Abraham's farmhand Jacobo put on his finest pair of bombachas –he was the most argentinized of the boys– and rode from house to house to announce a meeting at the synagogue. It was, of course, resolved not to work on the holiday, to decorate all the doorways with flags, and to hold an assembly at which Rabí Israel Kelner would deliver a speech. It was further decided to extend a special invitation to Don Benito Palas and to Herr Bergmann, the Chief Administrator, a gruff, unfriendly German who could not care less about Argentina's Independence Day.

A serious problem arose in the course of the preparations: No one knew the colors of the Argentine flag. But the plans were too far along to make any changes, so the work proceeded as scheduled.

When the great day arrived, Rachil was decked out like a ship about to be launched. Every doorway was awash in every which color –all except the colors of the flag. A warm sun shone over the countryside, transforming the yellow-hued bushes and shrubs into a carpet of gold. The small band sent over for the occasion by Don Benito struck up the notes of the national anthem; the immigrants may have been unsure about the exact meaning of the day, but their hearts overflowed with deeply-sensed joy.

Dressed in their finery, the men and women made their way to the synagogue for a service of thanksgiving. A sea of snow-white Jerusalem tunics sparkled in the sunlight as the slaughterer recited the solemn *Misha-berach* prayer.

The young people stood outside, chatting about their latest amorous adventures and going over plans for the upcoming dance. After the reading from Scripture, the mayor delivered the sermon. He was the least versed in rabbinic learning, but he had picked up enough snippets from the Talmud to give his words an authoritative ring. He was a skilled orator, and imitated the style of the synagogue preachers to great effect, poking his finger in the air and stroking his handsome brown beard.

"I remember," he said, "how after the massacre of Jews in the city of Elizabetgrad, we closed the synagogue because we didn't want to bless the czar. Here, no one is forcing us to bless the republic and its president; we do so gladly, of our own free will."

No one knew who the president was, but that did not matter very much.

After the festive luncheon the crowd gathered in the clearing, where the band, standing under a bower decorated with wild flowers, played the national anthem over and over. The young men showed off their horses, while the farmhands looked on and helped themselves to the homemade pies and pastries. Only the demijohn of wine remained untouched, waiting for the police chief to arrive.

At three, Don Benito Palas rode in with his escort, holding a large flag. The crowd broke into loud applause and the official ceremony began. Don Benito downed his glass of wine as Rabí Israel Kelner approached the podium. Speaking in the popular vernacular he saluted the country "where there were no massacres of Jews," and then launched into the parable of the two birds –a story that his neighbors had heard him tell countless times.

The parable, attributed to the talmudists of Segovia, taught a lesson about a people's right to freedom.

"There was once a bird imprisoned in an iron cage," Kelner began. "It thought that all birds lived in a cage, until one day it saw another bird flying in the wide open sky, soaring above the rooftops, flitting from branch to branch. The songbird became very sad when it compared its enslavement with the other bird's freedom. It resolved to break out, so every night it picked and picked at the hard metal bars. When it finally succeeded in flying away, its sad song turned happy, and soon it was soaring as high as all the other birds."

Jacobo explained the gist of Kelner's speech to Don Benito Palas, whose knowledge of talmudic symbolism was exceedingly meager. In response, Don Benito recited several stanzas of the national anthem. The Jews did not understand what he was saying, but the sound of the word "liberty" rekindled bitter memories of centuries of suffering. With their hearts and their mouths, just as they did in the synagogue, they responded with a resounding "Amen!"

Commemorative postcard for the Moisesville Centenial

Appendix: Two Stories (1936)

Dr. Nachum Yarcho, surrounded by settlers

The Miraculous Doctor

The young women of Rachil, Rosh Pinah, Espíndola, and San Gregorio, and the widow with the hazel eyes who lived on the outskirts of Carmel, were all upset to hear that a new doctor had settled in the colonies.

"Will he be like Dr. Richené?" the widow asked, as she smoothed her hair with one hand and with the other adjusted the rustling silk moiré sash whose purpose was to draw attention to her tiny waist.

Her question reflected the deep and lasting impression that Dr. Richené had made on the ladies. Whenever the good doctor came by to see a sick patient, they would stand in the doorways of their huts dressed to the nines, just to catch sight of him riding side-saddle on his chestnut horse. He sported a waxed mustache, a pith helmet worn at a jaunty angle, close-fitting linen trousers, and boots polished to a mirror shine.

How could the new doctor ever resemble Richené, who had a sweetheart on almost every farm, and two more in each of the train stops, not counting the girl in Colón whose house had balconies with brass railings? Would he at least be like the doctor's assistant at the hospital in Domínguez, that tall hulk of a man with a back as broad as a pile of corn in a good year, who gave candy to the women after barely listening to their chests, but who sometimes patted them in the wrong places with a little too much affection?

My cousin Chanyetze said:

"I'm sure he's a bachelor."

"No, he's probably married," Eva retorted. She was the

Eva who lived on the other side of the breakwater, who every winter was doomed to end the courtship she had worked so hard to begin during the summer harvest, when young workers abounded around the threshing machine.

"I've heard it said that his wife lives in Paris," Oxman's wife declared.

"In Paris?" the widow asked sighing. "In Paris? Then she must have her picture taken very often."

* * *

Nachum Yarcho disappointed the widow and disillusioned the girls. Instead of a helmet, he wore a slouch hat that invariably fell off his head the minute he sat down in his sulky, and in place of patent leather boots he wore canvas shoes with scandalously-delightful yellow leather toecaps. He did of course wear glasses –he was a doctor after all–, a pair of gold-rimmed spectacles that were always fogged up and always perched warily on his thin, hooked nose. If I may be permitted an anachronism, I will confess that Dr. Yarcho was hardly what we would today call a pure Aryan. On the contrary. Although he had studied in Russia and in Paris, and read books by Tolstoy, you were sure to find his diminutive figure standing by the synagogue door on Saturday mornings –mind you, with the same hat and the same shoes.

It was not that he was so strictly observant, or that he deprived himself of a smoke on the Jehovah's holy day. In point of fact Nachum Yarcho was somewhat of an epicure who broke the law with a smiling nonchalance. Then what was he doing in the synagogue while old Rubinstein raised his voice in fervent prayer, or the congregation was solemnly listening to chapters from the Pentateuch? He was doing what he did for most of his simple but memorable life:

telling stories and listening to stories being told. He was one of those extraordinary men you read about in novels of sorcery or poets' lives.

Yarcho delighted in talking to the hunched and wrinkled old ladies whose conversation was peppered with "Woe is mes" and "God bless yous," and who always knew the juiciest secrets in town. But most of all he liked to palaver with the old men, who discoursed liked seasoned talmudists and spiced their grave and curvilinear perorations with just the right dose of pungent wit –even when they could not quite tell the difference between the raised arms of an "Aleph" and the solemn portico of a square-shaped "Daled."[1] Theirs was a wit as rapid as their wink, as sharp as the pinch of snuff they invariably held between fingertips brown with smoke and the stain of phylacteries rubbed time and time again.

* * *

His first weeks in practice did little to enhance his reputation. The hospital assistant was particularly disconcerted. Dr. Yarcho did not prescribe any ointments or syrups –those reddish or greenish concoctions that all smelled the same but seemed to work better when they were in a fluted bottle rather than a smooth one. No, the good doctor was definitely not in the habit of handing out prescriptions, no matter how many heavy volumes he had piled up on his desk, or how many medical journals arrived from France. The slaughterer's wife was in a foul mood when she came back from Domínguez. Her trip had turned into a veritable expedition after a wheel on

---

[1] "Aleph": the first letter of the Hebrew alphabet; "Daled": equivalent to the letter "D"*(author's note)*.

the butcher wagon came loose. In her haste, she had decided to make the journey on a cart laboriously drawn by a team of meek and gentle oxen. They were a disciplined, reliable pair, responsive to commands in Yiddish, and particularly sensitive to strong curses in Spanish, but impossibly slow and short of gait, and determined to stop and nibble at every bush along the road to town.

Dr. Yarcho was delighted to see her.

"I was expecting you, ma'am," he said.

The slaughterer's wife was deeply touched. She was obviously in the presence of a wise doctor, who knew when his patients were coming even before they were announced. Of course, he would never bother to wait for Chaimovich's wife –a common so-and-so who dared to cook on the Sabbath, pinched the young men at all the weddings, and wore her corset so tight that it was a disgrace. No, he was expecting her, first cousin to the rabbi of Rosh Pinah, a woman so virtuous and dutiful that she had given birth to her last child at the same time that she was celebrating her silver wedding anniversary.

"So you were expecting me," she whispered after catching her breath and recovering from her shock.

"Yes I was," he repeated. "Until noon, I wait for the young women. Since they have nothing better to do, they come to my office before going to the store to look at fabric, ribbons, and lace."

"You're so right, doctor. Young women are such featherbrains. Take Chaimovich's wife, for example..."

"Then in the afternoon," Yarcho continued, "I wait for the serious ladies who come to tell me about their problems before going to the store to look at fabric, ribbons, and lace. But you, you don't do that sort of thing, do you? You know, you should really watch yourself."

"My God! Am I that sick, doctor?"

"No, not that sick. But you should take care. Who shouldn't?"

"Dr. Richené forbade me to eat meat."

He walked her over to the window. The immense, cropped plain was blazing in the sun. Rays of light bubbled in the crystal-clear air.

"Open your eyes wide. Do you see those clouds drifting by like rosy little lambs? Did you ever see clouds like that back in your rotten Russian village?

"I'm not in the habit of cloudwatching," she said. "I'm much too busy."

"Oh, but you should watch the clouds. Believe me, it's very good for your health."

"And what else do you advise me, doctor?"

"I advise you to eat a little meat, not to worry too much, and not to take any more medication; it's harmful to some people. What's your favorite dish? Meat wrapped in vine leaves? Stuffed fish? Potato pie with cracklings? Don't forget to invite me over if I'm in the neighborhood. Oh, and as for your leg, don't pay any attention to it."

"How do you know that my leg hurts?"

"What did the good Lord give us legs for, if not to hurt? Do you want proof? Just look at Don Isaac, the one from San Miguel. He never complains about his legs because he was born without any. So I ask you, isn't it better to have legs that hurt, than not to have legs that hurt, like Don Isaac?"

"It's incredible," she told her neighbors. "He didn't give me anything –not even syrup. It makes me wonder if he's really a doctor." Then she added in a confessional tone, almost as if she were commiting a sin: "The funny thing is, while he's talking, you're smiling. And the doctor's smiling too. You forget that he's the doctor. He just smiles and smiles and smiles."

* * *

The people of Rachil, Rosh Pinah, Espíndola, and San Gregorio were in a state of anxious anticipation. Not because of the drought, nor the rumors of an imminent revolution fueled by the presence in the Villaguay of a colonel from Paraná, nor the predictions of an invasion of locust. Something dramatic was about to occur: Hunchback María was expecting a baby. The same thing had happened last year, but after he examined her Dr. Richené became alarmed.

"Your wife can't have children," he announced to her husband.

Luckily, his diagnosis was premature. Doña María was then as far away from giving birth as she was now close. God's grace was with her; anyone could see it. Her little-monster looks inspired pity. With her perfect face, her dark and luminous eyes, and her timid, lilting voice she seemed to be begging forgiveness for existing in a world inhabited by women like the beautiful widow from Carmel. She inspired pity because that radiant face of hers tottered on an awful body –minute, miserable, misshapen.

"Dear God," she would moan. "What if my child looks like me..."

"If your child looks like you," Dr. Yarcho would calm her, "it will have your eyes and your voice, and it will sing like you. I'll let you in on little secret. God was my classmate at the University of Paris, and I can assure you that He knows exactly what He's doing. I know Him quite well."

And the hunchback would smile, smile with her eyes, smile with her hands –hands pale and translucent as if already cradling the head of the child suckling at her breast.

"She'll scream a lot, won't she, doctor?" Mrs. Mirner inquired. She had so many grandchildren and nephews that she held the unofficial title of midwife, and assisted in all the births.

"Why? Are you tired of the screaming?" Yarcho asked. "But what difference does it make to you? Don't you fall asleep between the screams? Tell me, have you heard about Benjamin Riber's divorce?"

"Who hasn't? Do you think I'm deaf? I don't like to go about repeating things, but Riber's a poor wretch. Imagine, on Passover his wife came to temple with rouge on her cheeks."

* * *

One Sunday evening the doctor's sulky was seen stopped in front of the hunchback's little house. It should be pointed out that she was called "the hunchback" not because she had a hump, but because it was the only thing she did not have. María was stretched out on the bed, quietly absorbed in thought. She smiled at the little man who was smiling down at her, and felt more at ease.

"What a beautiful room you have, María! It looks and sings like you, and it's going to have a baby, just like you."

Outside, along the broad street shaded by paradise trees, the people of Rachil paced and waited.

Birds, disturbed in their sleep, flitted from branch to branch. A black cat mewed on the rooftop; a dog barked at the moon –a full, round moon that followed travelers along the road and startled lovers kissing behind the harvesting machine. Dr. Yarcho came out to smoke a cigarette. The matrons surrounded him:

"How strange, doctor! She's not screaming."

"How do you expect her to scream on such a moonlit night? It would be a shame."

Jacobo, who in his fifteen short years had already acquired the reputation of a rascal and a first-rate rider and horse tamer, looked up at the lunar disk and tried to gain

Yarcho's confidence by asking astronomical questions:

"What's the moon made of, doctor?"

"Stearin and hardboiled eggs."

"Does the moon ever fall?"

"Every morning it falls into the Paraná River, and just before the stars come out the Big Fisherman upstairs fishes it out, and sets it rolling again. If you ever want to see it happening, go to Balvanera, climb up the eucalyptus tree, and wait there till dawn."

An owl hooted darkly in the shadows; a bat flew by, and the dog's barking once more cut through the silence. There was a muffled cry from the room, followed by a long, loud scream.

The doctor disappeared. As he closed the door behind him, two huge metal blades gleamed by the lamplight.

* * *

From that night on, Dr. Yarcho's name was uttered with reverential respect. People talked about his miraculous cures and his magical gift of gab. What was the source of his miracle working? No one could explain it, yet no one doubted it. Yarcho's fame spread from the humble and misty little Jewish farming villages to the large provincial cities. He was consulted from near and far; even the doctors of Villaguay and Gualeguay came to the hospital in Domínguez to get his opinion about their most difficult cases. One time, Dr. Pita, of the famous Córdoba Pitas, gave him the following advice:

"Dear colleague, you're making a big mistake by staying in these backwater towns. Go to Buenos Aires. You'll become rich and famous there."

"More famous than I am here? I doubt it. Here, everyone greets me and helps me fix my reins. I wonder what they use

to make reins over at Crespis. They're constantly breaking.
And as for being rich, let me tell you something –I already
am. I own twenty-three hectares of land, two pairs of shoes,
and my wife's just come back from Uruguay with a brand
new hat."

"Stop joking, doctor. Go to Buenos Aires, or at least to
Paraná. They'll make you a deputy within a year."

"Really? Thank you for telling me. I was planning to go
to Paraná next week, but after hearing what you've said, I'm
not so sure I'll go. And the governor's a friend of mine. You
can always trust a politician, of course..."

"Life's a big joke to you."

"No, my friend, it's serious business. What would I do in
Buenos Aires or in Paraná? In Buenos Aires and Paraná people suffer, they get tired, full of despair; they feel imaginary
aches and pains, and ignore the real pains that are eating
them up. It's exactly the same in Villaguay, in Domínguez,
in Rachil and in Las Moscas. Here, if my patients let me, I
can spend entire mornings sitting in the garden with a book
on my knees, right under the paradise tree where the larks
come to nest –I'm on intimate terms with larks, you know.
Have your big city doctors ever experienced such joys? Now
tell me, don't you love to watch bees?"

Pita thought for a moment:

"That must be why Maciá calls you a philosopher. That,
and the business about the little drink."

The story of the "little drink" was known far and wide. A
rancher from La Capilla once secretly came to consult
Yarcho. His son was becoming too fond of the bottle.

"I'm very worried, doctor, very worried. I don't know
where he gets it. I'm well over fifty, and I've never touched
a drop."

Yarcho jumped off his chair and roared toward the back
of the house:

"Guterman! Bring me that bottle of sherry!" He turned to the man and said: "You're not leaving here without a taste." The startled rancher mumbled:

"Doctor, I didn't know you drank!"

"I drink, eat, sleep, and ride around in a sulky," Yarcho responded.

"I would have never believed it."

"What's more, my religion demands it. The same religion that forbids me to eat pork commands me to bless wine. And since I don't know the blessings by heart I perform the ritual just by drinking the wine."

"That's fine and good. But if you drink too much..."

"I can't drink too much because I don't have enough time to get thirsty. Of course, we have to be careful about doing things to excess. Do you remember what happened to Israel Fachman? Poor man. He was so devout, so kindly. All he did from the moment he got up till the moment he went to bed was pray. He was praying when his hut burned down. Since that day, he's never prayed again. How's the sherry? I received it as a gift."

"From the governor?"

"No, the priest in Concordia sent it to me."

The mayor of Villaguay contributed to Yarcho's growing reputation as a philosopher with his colorful renditions of the doctor's adventures, and his stories about the times the sulky got stuck in the mud flats near the Vergara Creek. But he could make little sense of the ideas the doctor presented at a meeting called to consider major improvements to the town.

"It would be very simple to repair the plaza, the church, the town hall," he said. "Last Tuesday, I was coming back from Domínguez. My horse was bone tired, so I stopped to let him a rest. I looked down the road, and lo and behold, I saw a bright and shining city right before my eyes, with golden towers, golden domes, golden palaces, and golden trees. The doctor in that city must also ride a golden sulky, I said to myself, and continued on my way. Now I ask you: Couldn't we copy that lost city floating on the horizon? It's so foolish to copy ugly things. If I were elected mayor, I'd take the city I saw in the clouds and set it down in each corner of the plaza."

The gauchos called him at any hour of the day or night. Yarcho would travel for hours in his covered sulky to save a child suffering from diphtheria, to operate on a wounded man, to attend a poor servant girl turned away by the fancy doctors. He often rode into the grasslands around San Gregorio to treat the cattle rustlers and gauchos who had been a little too quick with the knife near Vásquez's general store. He would open his bag right in the middle of the miserable cane and tin hovels and give out whatever medicine was needed, so that the fugitives would not have to come to the dispensary and risk a run-in with the police.

Once, on his way to San Salvador, he was attacked by a band of marauders staking out a herd near the Escriña ranch. It was raining and thundering as it only can in Entre Ríos when the sky opens up. There was a sudden flash of lightening and Yarcho saw the muzzle of a blunderbuss pointed straight at the sulky.

"Tell me, González," Yarcho asked, "how's that arm of yours?"

"For God's sake, it's the doctor."

"Do me a favor, González," the unexpected traveler continued. "As long as you're here why don't you fix my reins?"

Everyone –the Jews, the gauchos, the women– praised his brilliant skills, his gentle wit, his smile, his stories. The women felt a special affection, and by now even the widow from Carmel had forgotten the incomparable Dr. Richené.

"My God, how that man smiles!" she exclaimed, as her heart fluttered wildly.

"And how he talks!" Aida chimed in; she was the Aida that everyone avoided because of the business with the fellow from the Benítez ranch. When that unmentionable "thing" happened, her mother came to see Yarcho.

"I'm brokenhearted, doctor, so brokenhearted. You know, my daughter..."

"Your daughter is the prettiest girl around; she's a wonderful girl."

"Yes, but instead of getting married... I'm so brokenhearted..."

"What do you mean she didn't get married? She got married in Diamante. I was a witness at her wedding. So was Sandoval. You know Sandoval, don't you?"

After the mother left, Yarcho told Guterman:

"Remember, Sandoval and I were the witnesses at the wedding. Luckily for us, the poor devil of a groom died in Uruguay, so he won't be able to say a thing. Neither will Sandoval, because we don't know who he is..."

Many years later, people still talked about Yarcho and his prodigious doings. The rabbi declared:

"He was a saint. I've never met a more deeply Jewish Jew."

The sheriff fingered his long scar and said:

"He was a great gaucho."

The women, the dear, wonderful, lovely women who know much more about human nature than either rabbis or sheriffs, whispered:

"How that man smiled, oh, how he smiled!"

And they smiled too. The women, the dear, wonderful, lovely women just smiled and smiled and smiled...

THE SILVER CANDELABRA

The hut was bathed in bright, clear sunlight, in the placid warmth of the autumn morning. From the open window set deep in the cracked adobe wall, you could see the countryside stretched out far into the distance, beyond the hill covered with yellow thistle and a solitary paradise tree. The cow stood near the house, and playfully licked her little calf's back.

It was the Sabbath; the colony was enveloped in a peaceful silence broken only by the occasional hum of a woman's singing. Gedalí was already wrapped in his white tunic and was lost in prayer when his wife came in. He motioned her not to interrupt him, so she stepped back outside without saying a word. Gedalí overheard her telling their daughter:

"I couldn't ask him because he's praying."

Gedalí was very devout. He was not so learned nor so distinguished in the debates that took place in the synagogue over difficult commentaries and obscure passages in the texts. He was mild mannered and had a soft, melancholy voice. His deep-set eyes, topped by bushy, ash-colored brows, radiated the sweet, timid look of a flickering flame.

His tall, thin body looked even longer as he stood facing east, lost in the thick folds of his floor-length tunic. Suddenly, Gedalí sensed that someone was spying on him through the window. Without interrupting his devotions he slowly turned his head to see if it was his neighbor, the former soldier who always liked to mock his piety. But no, it was not the neighbor, it was a stranger who was at that very moment reaching in through the window to steal the candelabra –the silver candelabra, the family's precious heirloom, the cherished object that attested to its illustrious lineage even amid the drabness of the immigrant's hut. It stood proud and majestic, its seven arched branches with their silvery rosettes shining as brightly as the lights of the ritual tapers. Gedalí did not interrupt his prayers; he shot a stern look at the intruder, and wove this warning in between the syllables of the holy words:

"Don't... It's the Sabbath... It's the Sabbath..."

That was all he could say without profaning his worship. The intruder stole the candelabra while Gedalí prayed on, swaying back and forth to the rhythm of the sacred verses. He concluded the benedictions with a sad and tired murmur. He then took a deep breath, as the sunlight bathed his emaciated face, his lined forehead, his scraggly, graying beard.

He folded the tunic carefully and put it away in the chest drawer. When his wife came in, Gedalí informed her calmly:

"They've stolen our candelabra..."

He took a slice of the bread set out on the table and began to eat, as he always did after praying. His wife screamed at him, bursting with anger:

"And where were you, you piece of..."

Without a glimmer of indignation, like someone fully convinced that he had done his duty, Gedalí replied:

"I warned him that it was the Sabbath..."

NAMES AND TERMS

Aljamiado (S): Spanish written in Arabic script.

Baruch ata Adonai (H): "Blessed art Thou Oh Lord": the opening words of Hebrew benedictions.

boleadoras (Sa): gaucho lariat with lead balls on one end thrown around an animal's legs.

bombachas (Sa): loose gaucho trousers fastened at the bottom.

caudillo (Sa): political-military leader.

cherba-le-chaim (Ha): from the Hebrew *tzaar baalei chaim*, literally, "pain of living things." The term alludes to Jewish teachings forbidding cruelty to animals.

criollo (Sa): native Argentine, belonging to the land. Also, the Spanish spoken in the Argentine countryside.

dayan (H): religious authority, judge.

estilo (Sa): type of Argentine folk music.

Gemara (A): literally, "completion." The part of the Talmud that provides commentary on the *Mishnah* (see below).

Halevi, Yehudah (H): twelfth-century poet who was a central figure of the Jewish Golden Age in Spain. Legend has it that Halevi, famous for his songs to Zion, was trampled to death by a Muslim horseman at the gates of Jerusalem.

Harey-at (H): "Behold, you are...". The opening words of the marriage pledge recited by the groom. The complete formula runs: "Behold, you are consecrated unto me with this ring according to the law of Moses and Israel."

ICA: Jewish Colonization Association, often also called by the colonists "la Jewish."

Jewish: see ICA.

Kabbalah (H): literally, "tradition." Refers to Jewish mystical doctrine.

Kishinev: Russian city. Site of two serious pogroms (1903, 1905) that resulted in large-scale Jewish immigration to the Americas.

machzor (H): prayerbook for the Jewish High Holidays.

Misha-berach (Ha): "May He who blessed...". Opening words of a benediction.

Mischnais (Ha): from the Hebrew *Mishnayot*, "repetitions." The first codification of Jewish law. Also known as *Mishnah*. Together with the *Gemara* it forms the *Talmud* (see below).

mate (Sa): popular beverage brewed from the dried leaves of a South American evergreen.

Moreira, Juan: Argentine gaucho, outlaw, and folk hero. The protagonist of several famous literary works.

quebracho (Sa): tree found on the pampa.

Rabí (S): medieval Spanish form of "rabbi," from the Hebrew, "my master." Gerchunoff uses the term to render *reb*, the Yiddish word for "mister," used with a man's first name.

Rashi (H): acronym for Rabbi Shelomo ben Yitshak. The leading Jewish commentator on the Bible and Talmud. Lived in the eleventh century.

Sana Toikef (Ha): from the Hebrew, "Let us declare the sanctity [of this day]." One of the central prayers of the Jewish High Holiday liturgy.

santuario (S): niche for a Christian saint's image. Gerchunoff uses the word to refer to the ark in the synagogue containing the scrolls of the Pentateuch.

Schummer: Pen name of Nahum Meir Shaikevitch (1849-1906), Yiddish author who wrote hugely popular novels for a mass readership. Several dealt with the history of the Jews in Spain. (Also spelled "Shomer.")

shel yod (Ha): from the Hebrew, "of the hand." The part of the phylacteries, a symbol of God's commandments, wound around the arm and hand during certain prayers.

slaughterer: translation of the Hebrew *shochet*. A person trained in the laws of Jewish ritual slaughter. Frequently served as lay rabbi and judge in communities without these functionaries.

taba (Sa): game of jackstones.

Talmud (H): literally, "learning." Collection of writings constituting Jewish religious law. It consists of the *Mishnah* and *Gemara* (see above).

tiger: "tigre" in the Spanish original (Sa). Argentine Spanish uses the word to refer to the jaguar.

Urquiza, Justo José: military-political leader of Entre Ríos province in the mid-nineteenth century.

vidalita (Sa): Argentine folk song.

Yeshivah (H): Jewish religious academy.

Yom Kippur (H): "Day of Atonement." The holiest day of the Jewish liturgical year.

Zeroim (Ha): from the Hebrew *Zeraim*, "seeds." The first of the six orders of the *Mishnah*. It deals with agricultural laws.

Key to the abbreviations:

A: Aramaic

H: Hebrew.

Ha: The author often renders Hebrew terms according to the pronunciation of Eastern European Yiddish-speaking Jews.

S: Spanish.

Sa: The text contains many words characteristic of Argentine Spanish.